Follow in Their Footsteps

FOLLOW IN THEIR FOOTSTEPS

Glennette Tilley Turner

ILLUSTRATED WITH PHOTOGRAPHS

COBBLEHILL BOOKS
Dutton New York

PHOTOGRAPH CREDITS

Charles R. Beck, 98; copyright © by The Birmingham News Company 1993, 95; Boston Athenaeum, 27; courtesy of Marion Coleman, 126; DuSable Museum of African American History (Lynard M. Jones, photographer), 131 (top); Jo Evelyn Grayson, 153; The Howard University Gallery of Art, 30; Library of Congress, 59, 162, 169; Baldwin Room, Metropolitan Toronto Reference Library, 80; National Archives, 13; National Archives of Canada, 74; courtesy NAACP Public Relations, 65; courtesy of the William Tucker Collection, North Carolina Central University, 106, 110, 112; Schomburg Center for Research in Black Culture, The New York Public Library, 6, 128, 149 (Andrew J. Figueroa), 142 (Kojo Kamau); copyright Scurlock Studio, 42; Swanay Productions, photographs by Beverly Swanagan, 46, 48.

The skits in *Follow in Their Footsteps* may be performed without permission if not given for profit. For any profit-making performances, permission must be obtained in writing from the Publisher.

Library of Congress Cataloging-in-Publication Data
Turner, Glennette Tilley.
Follow in their footsteps / Glennette Tilley Turner.
p. cm. Includes Index.
Summary: Brief biographies of ten African Americans including Carter
G. Woodson, Dorothy Height, Thurgood Marshall, Charlemae Rollins, and
Alex Haley. With a skit about each to be acted out.
ISBN 0-525-65191-8
1. Afro-Americans—Biography—Juvenile literature. [1. Afro-
Americans—Biography.] I. Title. E185.96.T84 1997
920'.009296073—dc20 96-19777 CIP AC

Published in the United States by Cobblehill Books,
an affiliate of Dutton Children's Books,
a division of Penguin Books USA Inc.,
375 Hudson Street, New York, New York 10014

Designed by Mina Greenstein
Printed in the United States of America
First Edition   10 9 8 7 6 5 4 3 2 1

To
my husband
my sons and their families
and my brother and his family

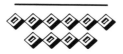

Contents

Introduction

As you read their stories, imagine that you are following in the footsteps of:

CARTER G. WOODSON, who felt that the contributions of Africans and African Americans should be better known, and did something about it.

EDMONIA LEWIS, whose artistic talent as a sculptress led to international acclaim.

DOROTHY I. HEIGHT, who knew the importance of family relationships and organized the first Black Family Reunions in cities across the United States.

THURGOOD MARSHALL, who as a lawyer and later as a Supreme Court Justice devoted his entire career to making the words "Equal Justice Under Law" apply to every American.

MARY ANN SHADD, who became North America's first black woman newspaper editor.

A. G. GASTON, who established numerous business enterprises and became a millionaire by "finding a need and filling it."

CHARLEMAE ROLLINS, whose love of books and children

made her an outstanding children's librarian and storyteller.

BESSIE COLEMAN, who earned an international pilot's license when few men and women of any race had ventured into the exciting new world of aviation.

ALEX HALEY, whose own family story, *Roots: The Saga of an American Family*, inspired others to seek out and appreciate their heritage.

MALCOLM X, who came to realize that change is possible, and that hopefully blacks and whites would one day live peacefully together.

Would you have been able to accomplish what these people did? Decide if you would have made the same decisions they did. Act out the skits about them, and use your imagination to make them as simple or as elaborate as you wish. Try to find other sources of information about the lives and work of these African-American achievers. When you realize that they succeeded against seemingly impossible odds, you will see new possibilities for realizing your own dreams.

Follow in Their Footsteps

CARTER G. WOODSON

CARTER G. WOODSON's life took some unexpected turns.

- He was born in a poor farming area of Virginia and never even saw a train before he was seventeen, but eventually traveled around the world.
- He never finished elementary school, yet he got a Ph.D. degree from Harvard University.
- He had no children of his own, but because he cared so much for children and their right to knowledge, he is remembered as the "Father of Black History."

The force behind these unexpected turns was Woodson's desire to discover information that had been kept secret and to share his discoveries with future generations. It all started because during the time when Carter Goodwin Woodson was in grade school, the books were missing a chapter. They never mentioned great things Africans and African Americans had contributed to America and the rest of the world. Woodson felt that something important was being hidden from him and all other American children. He felt that they were being deprived of information they deserved to know.

He had a chance to learn about this "hidden history" because he happened to have family members, friends, and teachers who helped him find out about it. This knowledge made him proud that people in his race had done a lot to build America. And knowing this made the young Carter G. Woodson feel that any child of any race who grew up not knowing of African-American achievements had an incomplete education. That child was denied a true view of American history. His goal was to do something about that situation.

Carter G. Woodson devoted so much time and effort to his work that he became known around the world as the "Father of Black History." He believed it was essential that the "chapter" which had been left out of his grade school books be included in the future. He set a goal for himself—to learn all he could about African-American history.

On September 9, 1915, Woodson and four other men, all highly respected in their professions, founded an organization. The cofounders were George Cleveland Hall, a doctor; W. B. Hartgrove, a teacher; Alexander L. Jackson II, a YMCA administrator; and James E. Stamps, a business executive and educator. The five men met in Mr. Jackson's office at the Wabash Avenue YMCA in Chicago. They called the new organization the Association for the Study of Negro Life and History. Its purpose was the collection and teaching of what had been "hidden history."

Carter G. Woodson spent his lifetime searching for ways to inform and inspire children. In 1926, he initiated the idea he is best remembered for. He encouraged schools to set aside the second week in February—near Abraham Lincoln's birthday

on the 12th and abolitionist Frederick Douglass' on the 14th—
to observe Negro History Week. The idea caught on immediately. What started as Negro History Week became Black
History Month in 1976. Today, the month of February is
African-American History Month. Mayors and governors and
the president of the United States issue proclamations stating
the importance of celebrating the life and history of African
Americans. The role of African Americans is being recognized
as a very significant part of American history as a whole, and
acknowledged throughout the year.

No one would have predicted this when Carter G. Woodson
was born on December 19, 1875. The Civil War had been over
ten years by then, and slavery had ended. At first, former
slaves like Carter Woodson's parents, James Henry Woodson
and Anne Eliza Woodson, had high hopes of being able to earn
a good living now that they were free. After all, they owned
land—a tobacco farm in New Canton, a town in Buckingham
County, Virginia. But they had a hard time providing the basic
necessities of life for Carter and his brothers and sisters—William, Robert Henry, Cora, Susie, and the baby Bessie. (Two
other children had died of whooping cough long before Carter
was born.) Their farm was in one of the poorest sections of
Virginia.

Even though Carter's parents were very poor, they valued
education highly. As slaves, they had been denied the chance
to learn to read and write. They believed that education was
the key to a good future and being able to earn a good living.
Yet they needed Carter's help on the farm and could not send
him to school regularly. He and his two older brothers took

Carter G. Woodson, who founded the Association for the Study of Afro-American Life and History.

turns going to school. His sister Cora got to attend school on a more regular basis.

School was held in the Baptist church across the road from the family's farm and was in session just five months a year because all farm children were needed to help plant and harvest crops. The teachers were Carter's uncles. His mother's brothers, John Morton Riddle and James Buchanan Riddle, took turns teaching in the one-room school. They taught the students what they knew of geography, spelling, arithmetic and United States history. And even when Carter wasn't able to attend school, he thought about the things he had learned. Whenever his uncles came to visit, Carter had lots of questions to ask them. As soon as Carter learned to read, his father would collect as many newspapers as possible and ask Carter to read to him. The newspapers were old ones, but gave information about world and national news. Carter continued to study on his own even when he wasn't in school.

New Canton was in a hilly section of Virginia near the James River where Carter sometimes went fishing. His father had worked as a carpenter during the time he was a slave. He had used his carpentry skills to build an addition on the house to provide for his growing family.

The Woodson family members felt close to one another. Carter's grandmother, Sarah Riddle, lived with them, and his uncles often visited. On summer evenings the adults enjoyed sitting on the porch and telling stories of their past experiences. The children enjoyed listening.

There were some stories that Carter especially liked to hear. One was about his mother, Anne Eliza, and his Grandmother

Sarah. Their master decided to sell some slaves to get money, and was going to sell Carter's grandmother. His mother was only a little girl at the time, but offered to be sold instead. Since the master could get more money for an adult, he sold her mother and two of her brothers, John and Robert. After the Civil War, the family was reunited. Even Robert, who had been carried away by Union soldiers, was back with them.

Another of Carter's favorite stories was about his father's escape from slavery. Because he was a skilled carpenter, he had made some fish traps and furniture to earn money for himself. He was beaten for it by his master, and he decided to leave before things got worse. He headed for Richmond where he had heard there were Union soldiers. When he spotted them, he was ordered at gunpoint to halt. He waved a white handkerchief to show that he wanted to surrender to them. They then welcomed him, and James Woodson became a soldier in the Union Army.

These stories and other details of Carter Woodson's life can be found in *Walking Proud* by Sister M. A. Scally. She notes that "The more Carter heard these stories, the greater was his pride in his family and the greater his desire to know more about the past. He longed to know about the faraway place called Africa that his people came from."

Carter's older brothers left home to get jobs. William became a coal miner in West Virginia, and Robert Henry soon joined him. When Robert came back to visit, he told stories about Huntington. People were saying that a high school for Negroes might be opening soon. That attracted Carter, and in 1892, he and Robert headed for Huntington. It was a railroad center, and the two worked for the Chesapeake and Ohio Railroad in Fayette County.

It wasn't long before Carter's parents decided to move to Huntington, West Virginia, too. James Woodson wasn't too enthusiastic about the move, but hoped it would improve their economic situation. When he and Anne Eliza and the two youngest children arrived in Huntington, Robert and Carter had given up their railroad jobs. There was more money to be made in the coal mines, and they went to Nutallburg to work in the same mine as their brother William.

Working in the mines was not only hard, it was hazardous. Carter was injured once by some falling slate. Constantly breathing coal dust caused many of the workers to have breathing problems. William developed a serious case of asthma and moved to Pittsburgh.

It was too far from the coal mine to go home for dinner, but Carter and Robert were able to get home-cooked meals nearby. Oliver Jones was an older miner who had been a cook before the Civil War. He turned his home into a restaurant, but the home-cooked food wasn't the only reason Carter Woodson liked going to Mr. Jones' house. Oliver Jones had his own library of books about achievements of African Americans. He himself had never learned to read, but when he found out that Carter could read, he made a deal with him. Carter could have anything he wanted to eat if he would read the newspapers and give Mr. Jones and his friends a daily news report.

Carter really liked this arrangement. He could keep up with current events, and listening to discussions of history and politics between Mr. Jones and his friends and being allowed to read the books was most educational. He dreamed of being able to attend the Frederick Douglass High School that had opened in Huntington. Three years after going to work in the mines, he was ready to enter high school. He was almost twenty years old.

With his help, his family had been able to buy a new house. Carter lived at home, and resumed his old practice of reading the newspaper to his father. He concentrated on his studies and finished high school in less than two years.

Most people living in 1897 would have considered a high school diploma to be enough education. In many places a high school graduate could be hired to teach elementary school. But Carter wasn't content to stop there. He had read of a college in Kentucky that had been founded by John G. Fee. Fee was from a Southern family that had held slaves, but he hated slavery. He started Berea College, which admitted black and white men and women. Every student was to be treated with respect as a human being. No one was to be treated as inferior or superior. Carter Woodson was impressed by what Berea stood for. He applied and got accepted.

Berea didn't give Woodson full credit for his high school work, but he didn't let that discourage him. By the end of the first year he was taking college level coures. At the end of the next year he returned to West Virginia and took a teaching job in Winona.

Being a teacher in those days meant doing everything, from making the fire to sweeping the floors, in addition to actually teaching. Carter was following this routine when he was asked to become the principal of Douglass High School in Huntington. He and his family were extremely proud of this honor. When he accepted the job, Bessie, his youngest sister, was just entering her senior year at Douglass. When she graduated, her big brother signed her diploma.

Woodson wanted to continue his studies and spent the summer of 1901 back at Berea. His goal was to attend the University of Chicago, and he was able to take a leave of absence to do so. He was greeted with the news that even after his work at Berea, he didn't have enough credits to enroll in graduate school. As usual, Carter Woodson worked things out. He took the necessary courses and received his Bachelor of Literature degree from Berea.

He wanted to earn a Master's degree at the University of Chicago, so resigned his job as principal of Douglass High School. He had just started the fall term when he received an appointment as an English teacher in the Philippine Islands. He couldn't resist taking advantage of this opportunity to travel and learn firsthand about people and places beyond the borders of the United States. He thoroughly enjoyed the new experiences, but the tropical climate did not agree with him. On his return trip he traveled around the world. He had begun to feel better after changing climates. He visited India and Malay where he was particularly interested in the educational system. He was eager to learn more about the history of Italy, Egypt, Palestine, and Greece. In Paris, he found the Bibliothèque Nationale to be a treasure trove of books on African history.

In 1908, Woodson received his Master's degree from the University of Chicago and entered the Ph.D. program at Harvard

University. He would need to write a major history research paper to get that degree, and in order to have access to an excellent library, he moved to Washington, D.C., to be near the Library of Congress.

His interest in African and African-American history was ongoing. He continuously pondered how he could find a way to provide schoolchildren with the chapter that had been missing from his grade school books. He and friends in Washington discussed a newly formed civil rights organization: The National Association for the Advancement of Colored People. W. E. B. DuBois, who had been the first African American to receive a Ph.D. from Harvard, was one of the founders of the NAACP and editor of their publication, *The Crisis*. Many of its goals were similar to the kinds of things Carter Woodson hoped to accomplish.

Woodson began teaching at the M Street High School in Washington. This enabled him to work with young people and to meet his living expenses. In 1912, he became the second African American to earn a Ph.D. in history. Soon after, his first book, *The Education of the Negro Prior to 1861*, was published and was a big success.

About this time a movie called "Birth of a Nation" was produced. It gave the impression that African Americans appear to be ignorant, and mean. Courageous black and white leaders spoke out against it as false teaching of history. Dr. Woodson knew that most children had grown up with little knowledge of the contributions of African Americans to the building of the United States or of the advanced civilizations of early Africa. He was convinced that the solution to this problem was

CARTER G. WOODSON

TEACHER, HISTORIAN, PUBLISHER

FROM 1903 TO 1906, DR. WOODSON WAS A SUPERVISOR OF SCHOOLS IN THE PHILIPPINES. HIS HEADQUARTERS WERE LOCATED NEAR THE SPOT WHERE THE FIRST JAPANESE FORCES LANDED AFTER PEARL HARBOR.

BORN OF EX-SLAVE PARENTS, YOUNG WOODSON COULD ONLY ATTEND SCHOOL ON RAINY DAYS, WHEN WORK ON THE FARM WAS IMPOSSIBLE. AT 17, HE WAS A MINER IN WEST VIRGINIA!

DR. WOODSON, THROUGH HIS SCHOLARLY WRITINGS, IS RESPONSIBLE, MORE THAN ANY OTHER SINGLE PERSON FOR FAMILIARIZING THE AMERICAN PUBLIC WITH THE CONTRIBUTION OF THE NEGRO TO WORLD HISTORY. HE IS THE ORIGINATOR OF NEGRO HISTORY WEEK, AND FOUNDER OF THE ASSOCIATION FOR THE STUDY OF NEGRO LIFE AND HISTORY. HIS WORKS ON NEGRO HISTORY ARE TO BE FOUND IN THE LIBRARIES OF EVERY IMPORTANT INSTITUTION OF LEARNING.

Alston for OWI

Carter G. Woodson as portrayed in Portraits in Black:
Charles Alston's Drawings of African Americans.

the forming of an organization to perpetuate the collection and teaching of accurate African and African-American history. The result was the September 9, 1915, meeting at which Woodson and the four other men established the Association for the Study of Negro Life and History.

Woodson was named Executive Director. He took the job very seriously. He had seen how well *The Crisis* magazine advanced the work of the NAACP and he decided—without taking the proposal to the Executive Board of the newly formed Association—to start a publication. He called it *Journal of Negro Life and History*. It made the Board members angry, but delighted readers, who were eager to have such a welcome source of information. Woodson firmly believed that it was essential that the Association keep publishing the *Journal*. He said, "In this way only can the Negro escape the awful fate of becoming a negligible factor in the thought of the world."

Carter Woodson worked tirelessly to help make this organization succeed. In addition to producing the *Journal*, mostly for adults, he began publication of the *Negro History Bulletin*, especially for students. But Dr. Woodson realized that the short articles in the *Bulletin* could not take the place of full-length books. Under his direction, the Association formed a book publishing company known as Associated Publishers, Inc. He personally wrote many books for young readers and encouraged other writers to do the same.

Carter Goodwin Woodson died in 1950 at the age of seventy-five. The *Journal* and the Association, now retitled the Association for the Study of Afro-American Life and History, continue Dr. Woodson's life's work.

A Walking History Lesson

CAST

Dr. Carter G. Woodson   Jeanette
Jerald   Jamella
Jackie   First Narrator
Juanita   Second Narrator

FIRST NARRATOR: This skit is based in part on an account which appears in *Walking Proud: The Story of Dr. Carter Goodwin Woodson* by M. A. Scally and published by Associated Publishers.

SECOND NARRATOR: It began one warm fall evening on the front steps of 1538 Ninth Street, N.W., Washington, D.C. This was where Dr. Carter G. Woodson lived, and where the offices of the Association for the Study of Negro Life and History were located.

FIRST NARRATOR: Dr. Woodson is greeted by a group of neighborhood children who know that every evening about this time he walked down the street to have supper at the cafeteria in the Phillis Wheatley YWCA.

SECOND NARRATOR: As he steps out of the building the children say:

ALL THE CHILDREN: Good evening, Dr. Woodson.

DR. WOODSON: Hello, there. How is everybody tonight?

ALL THE CHILDREN: Fine.

JERALD: What story are you going to tell us tonight, Dr. Woodson?

DR. WOODSON: What story would you like to hear? Do you want a story about Africa or America?

JACKIE: Either one.

JEANETTE: I know what story I want. I want to hear the one about the lady that YWCA is named for.

JAMELLA: Yes, tell us about Phillis Wheatley.

DR. WOODSON: All right. Phillis Wheatley's story is a story about both Africa and America.

JUANITA: Oh, good!

DR. WOODSON: But before I start the story, wouldn't you like an ice cream to be eating as you listen?

FIRST NARRATOR: Jamella said . . .

JAMELLA: Oh, yes!

SECOND NARRATOR: . . . as if stopping for ice cream wasn't part of their regular ritual.

FIRST NARRATOR: Two children held Dr. Woodson's hands and the others skipped along beside him as they went to the store.

SECOND NARRATOR: After all the children got their cones, the little group continued on toward the YWCA.

DR. WOODSON: Now, I'm going to tell you this story. And as soon as I finish, I want you children to run right on home before dark and to be sure to do your homework.

ALL THE CHILDREN: Yes, sir, we will.

DR. WOODSON (*looking down the street toward the "Y" building*): Does anybody already know something about Phillis Wheatley?

JERALD: Didn't she write poems?

DR. WOODSON: Yes, she did.

JACKIE: Wasn't she a slave? I heard that slaves weren't allowed to learn to read and write.

DR. WOODSON: Yes, she was a slave. And it's true, most slaves were forbidden to learn how to read and write, but Phillis' story was unusual.

JUANITA: How?

DR. WOODSON: In 1761, Phillis Wheatley was a little girl—about your age, Jamella. She was living a happy life with her family in Africa—probably Senegal in West Africa. The weather there was warm and sunny. One day Phillis was outdoors playing when she saw some men walking toward her.

JACKIE: She should have run!

DR. WOODSON: Yes, she should have, and she may have tried to. Being a little child, it is unlikely she could have run fast enough to get away. And it may be that since all the people she knew were kind to her, she may not have been afraid.

JEANETTE: What did the men do?

DR. WOODSON: They took her away with them.

JUANITA: That was kidnapping!

DR. WOODSON: Yes, it was.

JAMELLA: What did they do to her then?

DR. WOODSON: They took her to a schooner, which is a type of ship. She and many other African men, women, and children were chained to the lower deck.

JEANETTE: Why would they put chains on a little girl?

DR. WOODSON: To keep her fastened down.

JERALD: Dr. Woodson, you said she was on a ship. Where did the ship go?

DR. WOODSON: After about three stormy weeks on the Atlantic Ocean, it arrived in America. As you know, ships are given the names of women or girls. *Phillis* was the name of the ship that brought young Phillis to these shores.

JAMELLA: Was she named after that ship?

DR. WOODSON: Many people think so.

JACKIE: That was mean. But let's get back to the story. Where did the ship land when it got to America?

DR. WOODSON: It docked in the harbor at Boston, Massachusetts.

JERALD: Boston! Boston's up North. Did they have slavery in Boston?

DR. WOODSON: Yes, during the Colonial period they did.

JACKIE *(to the other children)*:   Will you all stop asking all these questions and let Dr. Woodson get on with the story! *(Then, turning to Dr. Woodson, Jackie said)*: What's the next thing that happened to Phillis?

DR. WOODSON: She was placed on an auction block in front of a large crowd of people.

JERALD: What's an auction block? And why were all those people there?

DR. WOODSON: An auction block is like a box or raised platform where the people who were going to be sold into slavery were forced to stand. Standing on the block raised them high enough that they could be seen by people in the crowd who had come to purchase slaves.

JACKIE: Wasn't Phillis too young to be a slave?

DR. WOODSON: I wish that was the case. But many babies were born into slavery if their parents were enslaved. Phillis was about your age. She was very thin and, I'm sure, exhausted after her trip.

JAMELLA: I bet when she looked out at all those people, she was so scared! I know I would be.

DR. WOODSON: I'm sure she was. Everything she saw was very strange and new.

JERALD: Well, did anybody buy her?

DR. WOODSON: Yes, she was purchased by John Wheatley, a man who ran a tailoring business. He was looking for a maid for his wife, Susannah.

JAMELLA (who was still thinking about Phillis' name):   So that's how she got her last name. The people who bought her were Wheatleys. I wonder what her real name was back home in Africa.

JACKIE (who was thinking about the fact that Mrs. Wheatley wanted a maid):   Phillis was too young and weak to be anybody's maid. She wasn't old enough to take care of her own self.

DR. WOODSON: The Wheatleys soon realized that and cared for Phillis almost as if she was a member of their family. She ate at the table with the family except when they had company.

JEANETTE: Except when they had company . . . so they didn't treat her just like they would have treated their own child.

JERALD: Did they have other slaves? How did they treat them?

DR. WOODSON: Yes, they did have other house slaves, and they were treated more like servants than family members.

JUANITA: How did Phillis like them?

DR. WOODSON: She liked them very much. She was especially close to an older slave woman whom the Wheatleys called "Aunt Sukey." She was like a grandmother to Phillis.

JAMALLA: I know she would have rather been in Africa with her real grandmother.

DR. WOODSON: I'm sure she would have far preferred that—and to have kept her freedom. But when you compare Phillis' life to that of other slave children, she did not experience as many physical hardships. In fact, Phillis quickly learned to speak the English language and Mrs. Wheatley taught Phillis to read. Many slaveholders thought that was wrong.

JUANITA: Why? Everyone should learn how to read!

DR. WOODSON: Yes, but most slaveholders feared that if slaves learned to read, they might read something that would give them the idea that they ought to be freed.

JACKIE: See, I told you it was against the law for slaves to learn to read.

DR. WOODSON *(smiling because Jackie had been the one who hadn't wanted the other children to interrupt the story)*:   Anyway, to get back to Phillis' story. Phillis could soon read well enough to read the hardest parts of the Bible.

JAMELLA: And there are some big words in the Bible.

DR. WOODSON: Not only did Mrs. Wheatley teach Phillis to read, the Wheatleys' eighteen-year-old twins also took an interest in teaching Phillis. It wasn't long after Phillis had learned to read that she began writing poetry. The Wheatleys were amazed.

JERALD: Why would they be so amazed, if she could do all those other things?

DR. WOODSON: Well, many slaveholders had tried to think of excuses for enslaving black people. They made up all kinds of reasons, that they weren't smart or were not as good as white people.

JACKIE: Anybody that believed that wasn't very smart himself.

DR. WOODSON: That's true, but at that time the idea was so widespread that when Phillis wanted to get some of her poetry published, she had to go to the Massachusett Governor's mansion to be quizzed by a group of prominent white men. They asked her all kinds of questions to test her to make sure she was intelligent enough to have written her poems!

JERALD: How did she do on the test?

DR. WOODSON: Superbly! She was magnificent, and the men were all happy to sign a paper stating that she was most highly capable. Soon after that Phillis had an opportunity to travel to England where the Countess of Huntington entertained her in her castle and treated her royally in every way. The countess had read some of Phillis' poetry and knew what a talented young lady she was.

JAMELLA: Wow! Phillis must have felt like a princess to live in a castle!

DR. WOODSON: I'm sure she did, and what's more, the countess had a book of Phillis' poems published. The book contained the statement that the prominent men had signed to remove all doubt that his young African woman had written the book herself. Phillis thus became one of the first American women to publish a volume of poetry.

FIRST NARRATOR: Realizing that the little group had reached the YWCA . . .

SECOND NARRATOR: . . . and that it was starting to get dark, Dr. Woodson says:

DR. WOODSON: We'll need to stop now, so you children can run along home. I don't want your parents to be worried about you or to say you can't walk me to the "Y" tomorrow evening.

FIRST NARRATOR: The children wave good night. Even the slowest eaters have finished their ice cream. They told Dr. Woodson:

ALL THE CHILDREN: See you tomorrow . . .

SECOND NARRATOR: As Dr. Woodson stepped inside the YWCA, he could hear one of the children saying, "Tomorrow I'm going to ask him to tell us a story about . . ."

Edmonia Lewis

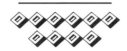

EDMONIA LEWIS was the first person of color to gain international fame as a sculptor. One of her sculptures was an award winner at the 1876 Philadelphia Centennial Exhibition which displayed 100 years of American creativity with that of other nations. American and European tourists flocked to her art studio in Rome. Pope Pius IX visited her there.

Edmonia had not set out to be a sculptor. Her decision grew out of an experience she had soon after she moved from Oberlin, Ohio, to Boston in 1863. She was so impressed when she first saw a life-sized statue in front of the Boston City Hall that she immediately decided she wanted to become a sculptor. Within a year she had received some instruction and became confident enough in her ability that she opened her own studio. Two years later she sailed for Italy, where she confidently established a studio as a sculptor. Although many miles from home, she chose to depict themes from her African-American and Chippewa-Indian heritage. She was praised for her "great natural genius, originality, earnestness, and genuine taste."

Surprisingly little is known about certain details of Edmonia Lewis' life. This is partly because she seemed to delight in keeping the public guessing, and partly because records were not kept. She said she was born in 1844 near Albany, New York. Some writers, however, claim that she was born in 1843 or 1845. What is known is that Edmonia Lewis' name was originally Wildfire. The name perfectly described her zest for life.

Her father was a black freedman who worked as a "gentleman's gentleman." Her mother was a Chippewa Indian woman who, with her kinspeople, sold handmade items in cities around Niagara Falls. Both parents died when Edmonia was very young. She was raised by her mother's sisters.

Throughout her life, Edmonia cherished memories of childhood. She had enjoyed fishing, swimming, making bead baskets and embroidered moccasins to sell. As an adult, she felt she had probably inherited her creativity. She recalled that her mother had had a talent for creating beautiful designs for embroidery. "Perhaps the same thing is coming out in me," she said.

Edmonia Lewis had an older brother whose name was Sunrise. He was a pivotal person in her life. Many of the things she did were made possible by his guidance and support. Sunrise had attended Indian school and later joined the California gold rush. Being a gold miner, he was able to pay for Edmonia to attend a grade school near Albany, New York. However, her first school experience was an unhappy one.

When she was about fourteen her brother returned from California. He took her by stagecoach from New York to Ohio where he enrolled her in the high school preparatory department of Oberlin College. It was at Oberlin that she changed her name from Wildfire to Mary Edmonia Lewis. Later, she dropped the Mary.

Oberlin, Ohio, had a reputation as a safe haven for black people fleeing from slavery. Oberlin College had a reputation as an excellent school. When it was founded it was the first coeducational college in America. A few years later it became the first college to welcome African-American students.

When Edmonia Lewis first arrived, she didn't take herself seriously as a student. Before long, though, she was doing well in such difficult subjects as Latin and Greek. She did not study sculpture, but she may have taken a drawing class. She drew a picture as her wedding present to a classmate.

She had an open, cheerful personality and made friends easily. She and twelve other girls lived in the home of the Reverend John Keep, the college trustee who had cast the vote that decided that Oberlin would enroll African-American students.

Edmonia got along well with the other girls who lived at Reverend Keep's home. However, she was involved in a mysterious incident concerning two of the girls. One winter holiday the girls were preparing to take a sleigh ride to their hometowns. Edmonia offered them a warm drink before they started out, and both girls got sick on the way home. There was speculation that their illness may have been caused by the drink Edmonia had served. The girls recovered, and that probably would have ended the incident but some townspeople who blamed her beat her up. There was a hearing to decide whether Edmonia was guilty or innocent of the charges. Her lawyer was Oberlin graduate John Mercer Langston who, like Edmonia

Lewis, had African and American Indian ancestry. He later became the first black person to win elective office in the United States. All charges against Edmonia were dropped because of lack of evidence. Her friends happily carried her from the courtroom on their shoulders.

When Edmonia left Oberlin, she went to Boston. There she soon met artists, abolitionists, and other social reformers. Her interest in art quickly surfaced. "I had always wanted to make forms of things; and while I was at school I tried to make drawings of people and things," she said.

It was at Boston City Hall that she was inspired by the life-sized statue that sculptor Richard Greenough had made of Benjamin Franklin. Seeing it, she knew that she *had* to become a sculptor. This was a field in which relatively few women and no African-American men or women had gained wide recognition. Being a pioneer did not discourage Edmonia Lewis. One of the first people she met in Boston was William Lloyd Garrison, an abolitionist and something of a pioneer himself. He was editor of the *Liberator*, a newspaper dedicated to putting an end to slavery.

Garrison introduced Edmonia to a local sculptor by the name of Edward Brackett. Brackett had done a portrait bust of John Brown. Knowing that John Brown had given his life to help free her father's people from slavery made Edmonia Lewis respect Brackett for his choice of subject. She studied with him for a time.

Brackett started Edmonia Lewis out with the sculpture of a baby's foot. When he examined the clay copy she made, he was impressed by her serious effort and her talent. He made

Sculptor Edmonia Lewis

a few suggestions, and she worked until every detail was exactly right.

With money her brother provided, Edmonia opened a studio. It was in the Studio Building at 89 Tremont Street. She hung a sign above her door: "Edmonia Lewis, Artist." Edward Mitchell Bannister, an established black landscape painter, maintained his studio in the Studio Building. Reportedly, he helped the fledgling young sculptor by acquainting her with art patrons. Anne Whitney was another artist with a studio in the building on Tremont Street. She was noted for a sculpture entitled "Africa," which depicted an African woman awakening from the nightmare of slavery. She had been a sculptor for ten years and had been denied entrance to a school where she hoped to study anatomy because that school only admitted men.

Edmonia Lewis quickly established herself. She won praise for modeling the likenesses of abolitionists such as William Lloyd Garrison, Charles Sumner, and Wendell Phillips. However, her sculpture of war hero Col. Robert Gould Shaw was her secret to success. The Civil War was drawing to a close. Shaw had died leading the 54th Massachusetts Volunteers, the first black regiment from a free state, and was from a prominent Boston family. Shaw was a hero to Bostonians and making an acceptable bust of him would be the true test of a sculptor's skill.

Edmonia Lewis felt she was equal to the task. She had gotten a glimpse of Shaw when he rode through Boston with his troops, and studied photographs of him. The bust she made pleased his family so much that they bought it immediately.

She made and sold one hundred copies of the Shaw sculpture, and used the money from these sales to sail to Europe on August 26, 1865.

She visited London, Paris, and Florence, Italy. In Florence, she met Hiram Powers, one of the most successful American sculptors in Italy. With its abundance of marble and the availability of artisans to carve it, Italy had a special appeal to sculptors.

Edmonia settled in Rome and opened her own studio there. She was eager to get to work. She donned a red fez and began creating marble statues. The little red velvet cap became her hallmark.

She was faced with all the challenges of making the transition from working in plaster and clay to working with stone. Edmonia Lewis felt an additional personal challenge. She knew that some critics still had to be convinced of the abilities of a black Indian woman. Instead of hiring Italian artisans to carve the statues once the model had been made, Edmonia did the carving herself. She feared that her work would not be considered original otherwise.

Being small in stature but determined to do all the work herself limited the number of pieces Edmonia Lewis could produce. Once she established herself, she hired artisans to carve her work into marble. She did the finishing.

Edmonia was not the only American woman artist attracted to Rome. The group included sculptor Harriet Hosmer, actress Charlotte Cushman, and Anne Whitney joined them the following year. Most sculptors in Italy at that time had adopted a neoclassical style, that is, they made their sculptures look

"Forever Free" by Edmonia Lewis

very much like the ancient Greek and Roman sculptures. At first, Edmonia Lewis' work was naturalistic and she was praised by some American art critics for her fresh approach. Later, she blended her naturalistic style with the popular neo-classic style.

Her work attracted a lot of attention. American and European tourists flocked to her studio near the Piazza Barbarini. Visitors included Pope Pius IX and Gen. Ulysses S. Grant.

The first sculpture she executed in Italy was of an African-American mother and child. It was called "The Freed Woman and her Child." Technically, this was an ambitious undertaking because sculpting two figures is more difficult than doing just one. That first statue was soon followed by what is perhaps Edmonia Lewis' most famous sculpture, "Forever Free." It shows a man and woman expressing the joy they felt when they were emancipated from slavery. Edmonia explained, "My first thought was for my . . . father's people, how I could do them good in my small way."

Next, Edmonia did some sculptures which paid tribute to her Indian ancestry. "The Wooing of Hiawatha" and "The Marriage of Hiawatha" were inspired by Henry Wadsworth Longfellow's poem. Longfellow was the most popular American author in Europe at that time. He visited Rome in 1869, and Edmonia got his brother to bring him to her studio where he sat for a portrait bust. Edmonia's sculpture of Longfellow is now part of the Harvard University Portrait Collection.

Edmonia also depicted a biblical character with "Hagar in the Wilderness." By the early 1870s, her work was sought after by art patrons on both sides of the Atlantic Ocean. Dr. Harriet

K. Hunt wanted a monument for her cemetery plot and commissioned a statue of Hygeia, the Greek goddess of health. It still stands in Mount Auburn Cemetery in Cambridge, Massachusetts.

Edmonia Lewis made several trips back to the United States to show and sell her work. In the summer of 1870, she exhibited "Hagar in the Wilderness" in Chicago. One report said it sold for $6000, another that the price was $3000. Either was much more than the eight dollars she had sold her first sculpture for. In 1873, she visited California and took five pieces to be exhibited by the San Francisco Art Association. Two of the works sold, and Edmonia took the three remaining pieces to San Jose. One was a bust of Abraham Lincoln, the others were her lighthearted statues of babies called "Asleep" and "Awake." These three pieces are still owned by the San Jose Library.

When Edmonia Lewis was in the United States, she traveled extensively by train. Reportedly, African Americans, some of whom had very limited incomes, helped pay for her travels. They were not able to afford to buy expensive marble sculptures, but the belief persists that Edmonia made a sculpture of the black orator, Frederick Douglass, in more affordable terracotta (clay).

The Philadelphia Centennial Exposition in 1876 attracted artists from all nations. Thousands of works were exhibited, and at least six were by Edmonia Lewis, who was still in her early thirties. One of her sculptures, "The Dying Cleopatra," won an award. It was twelve feet high, weighed 4,000 pounds, and had taken four years to execute. One critic called it "very original and striking." Another considered it "the grandest statue in the Exposition."

Landscape painter Edward Mitchell Bannister, whose studio had been in the same building in Boston as Lewis's, received a bronze medal at the Exposition. The recognition he and Edmonia Lewis received was an important milestone for them as individuals and for their race.

Much of Edmonia Lewis' work has been lost. One piece that had been thought lost has reappeared. "The Dying Cleopatra" was bought by the International Art Association of Chicago, then vanished. For more than 100 years, art experts believed it was lost, possibly destroyed. Then it turned up. A suburban Chicago fire chief was surprised to find it in a storage yard. For a time the Forest Park (Illinois) Historical Society adopted the statue, then officially transferred it to the National Museum of American Art, Smithsonian Institution.

The largest concentration of Edmonia Lewis' work is in Washington, D.C., at Howard University and the National Museum of American Art. Tuskegee University in Alabama has a piece; the Chicago Historical Society has some fragments of a sculpture.

Little is known of Edmonia Lewis' last years. According to some reports, she died in Rome about 1900. However, her biographer, Marilyn Richardson, found her signature in the guest book for a reception at the U.S. Embassy in Rome in 1909. She was also listed in directories published there in 1909 and 1911.

Certain details of Edmonia Lewis' life may never be known. What is known is that she was creative, courageous, and pioneering. Her work is her legacy.

The Treasure in Grandma's "Everything Room"

C A S T

Faye	C. J.
Phyllis	Narrator
Angela	

SCENE 1

NARRATOR: This is the day after the Smith family reunion. Most of the relatives have gone back to their homes, but two sisters, Faye and Phyllis, and Faye's children, Angela and C. J., have stayed to close up the old family home for the last time. The house is soon to be torn down to make way for a new road. We find the four of them at the breakfast table.

FAYE *(to Phyllis)*: Well, I guess we better get started. We've got a big job ahead.

PHYLLIS: Sure do. I have mixed feelings about closing up the house.

FAYE: Me, too.

PHYLLIS: I sure wish the house had been strong enough to withstand being moved to another location.

FAYE: So do I, but at least we can enjoy old memories as we go through things.

PHYLLIS: You know where I'd like to start . . .

FAYE *(laughingly completes the sentence)*:   . . . in the "Everything Room"!

ANGELA: The "Everything Room"? What's that?

FAYE: Our grandma—who was your and C. J.'s great-grandma— had a secret room which seemed to contain everything.

PHYLLIS: We used to come and visit in the summertime.

FAYE: If we wanted something to play with, Grandma would step into the room and come out with a little red wagon.

PHYLLIS: If it rained, Grandma would bring out raincoats that were just the right size.

FAYE: She didn't just have stuff for kids. If anybody in the family needed anything, Grandma would momentarily disappear into that room and bring out what was needed.

C. J.:   Where is this Everything Room?

PHYLLIS: Just off Grandma and Grandpa's bedroom.

FAYE: The door has a skeleton key that was always in the lock— but nobody other than Grandma, or occasionally Grandpa, ever went in there.

PHYLLIS: Not even our parents or aunts and uncles.

ANGELA: Why?

C. J.:   I bet she had something in there she didn't want anyone else to see.

ANGELA: You think so?

PHYLLIS: No, she just had practical kinds of things family members might need.

FAYE: I think her reason for making it "off limits" was that she had everything arranged so she could find whatever she wanted, and she was afraid things would get misplaced if she let everybody go in there.

ANGELA: Unless C. J. is right—and Grandma had something else in that room that she wasn't ready for the family to see.

C. J.:   I bet there's a hidden treasure in there.

PHYLLIS *(as the four of them walk toward the Everything Room)*:   Well, instead of guessing, let's go see what's in that room.

NARRATOR: Faye unlocks the door. Phyllis puts her arms around Angela and C. J. They all step into the room and say:

FAYE, PHYLLIS, ANGELA, and C. J.:   Wow!

SCENE 2

NARRATOR: The Everything Room is filled with boxes. They are stacked from the floor to the ceiling, and each is carefully labeled to indicate what it contains. But there is something quite different in the center of the room: a sawed-off tree trunk about three feet tall with an object on top of it.

ANGELA *(pointing to the object)*:   What's that?

PHYLLIS: I'm not sure, but it looks like a sculpture covered with a protective cloth.

FAYE: Why would Grandma keep a sculpture in here?

PHYLLIS: I can't imagine.

C. J.:   Can I take the cloth off?

PHYLLIS: Yes. I'm as curious as you are to see what's underneath.

FAYE *(to C. J.)*:   Here, let me help you.

C. J. *(who walks around the statue as he speaks)*:   It looks like a man's head made out of clay.

ANGELA: That man is Frederick Douglass. I'd recognize him anywhere. I wrote a paper about him in school.

C. J. *(standing at the back of the statue)*:   Uh-oh. There's some writing back here, but the letters don't spell "Frederick." They are E-D-M-O-N-I-A L-E-W-I-S.

ANGELA: That spells Edmonia Lewis.

FAYE: Edmonia Lewis!

PHYLLIS: I've read that she might have made some clay busts of Frederick Douglass, but I never dreamed our grandparents owned one!

FAYE: That is remarkable, isn't it?

C. J.:   Who's Edmonia Lewis? And what's a bust?

FAYE *(explains)*:   Edmonia Lewis was an outstanding black woman sculptor who lived way back in the 1800s. Not many of her sculptures are still around. Each one is worth thousands of dollars. A bust is the upper part of the human body, the head and shoulders.

ANGELA: So this really *is* a treasure, isn't it?

PHYLLIS: Yes, definitely.

ANGELA: But we don't have to sell it, do we?

FAYE: No, our grandparents surely wanted our family to have this as a gift to be handed down from one generation to another.

PHYLLIS: The fact that it was in the Everything Room proves that. They knew that eventually some family members would be curious to see what was in that room.

ANGELA: I'm glad it was us.

C. J.:   And I'm glad I predicted we'd find a treasure in the Everything Room.

DOROTHY I. HEIGHT

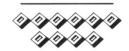

GOING TO A FAMILY REUNION is fun. Relatives come from near and far. You're greeted and hugged and kissed by everyone. You see cousins and aunts and uncles you may not have seen for years. You meet the new babies and brides and grooms that have come into the family since the last reunion.

You get a whiff of the good feast that awaits you. Maybe it's a barbeque. Certainly there will be an endless assortment of pies and cakes or perhaps peach cobbler for dessert.

One of the highlights of a family reunion is getting to hear family stories. You learn many things about your family and your heritage. You hear about hardships, triumphs, disappointments. You learn your responsibilities as a family member. If you are an African American, you may learn of the great civilizations that flourished in Africa where your ancestors came from.

Dorothy I. Height knew the magic of these sights, smells, and stories when she got the idea of having a Black Family Reunion. She knew that while families of all races enjoy getting together and getting better acquainted, this reunion would be especially meaningful. It would give many African Americans the opportunity to be reconnected with their extended family.

During slavery, parents and their children were often sold away from each other. After slavery ended, family members often moved away from the farms or small towns to find work in the big cities. Some went to work on the railroads. Some headed West to find a better life.

Over the years many family members lost touch with one another. Some were not as successful as they had hoped and did not want to let family members know. Others were busy with new jobs and new friends. Often there was no reason to go back home if their parents had died or the family home had been sold.

Understanding how many African Americans had lost touch with their own families, Dorothy Height started making plans for a Black Family Reunion. It would be similar to traditional family reunions and would foster a feeling of kinship and belonging. The first Black Family Reunion was held in Washington, D.C., in 1986. More than 200,000 people gathered on the Mall for a day of fun, information, and inspiration. Each person felt cared about and connected—whether or not he or she had a job, money, or an education.

There were large tents, or pavilions, with a variety of programs. Topics included storytelling, dance, music, the contributions of black people to America and the rest of the world. The people who attended that first Reunion loved being there. They started looking forward to the next year, and thinking of other family members and friends they could bring with them. Later, there were regional celebrations in big cities across the United States and a national celebration in Washington, D.C.

By 1990, the Black Family Reunions were attended by more than a million people.

After every Reunion, the National Council of Negro Women collects comments from people who attend. As a result of the Reunions there is the Excellence in Teaching Award and the Black Family Reunion cookbook.

People who had known and worked with Dorothy Height were not at all surprised that she would come up with such a creative idea, nor were they surprised by the success of the Reunion.

Much of Dorothy Height's ability to organize groups of people was learned during her childhood. She was born in Richmond, Virginia, on March 24, 1912. Her father, James Edward Height, was a building contractor. Her mother, Fannie Burroughs Height, was a nurse. When Dorothy was four, her family moved to Rankin, Pennsylvania, a town near Pittsburgh.

Both her parents had leadership positions in the black Baptist church there. Her father was the choirmaster and Sunday school superintendent. Her mother did a lot of work in the missionary society. Dorothy "sort of followed her around and got the idea of organizing clubs."

Dorothy was naturally shy, but did not let that keep her from being an excellent student. Her mother told her to always do her best rather than measure herself against anyone else. She was five feet nine inches tall at age eleven and played center on the girls' basketball team. She won spelling bees, debates, and essay contests. She was also active in youth groups at church.

Although Dorothy lived in the North and attended inte-

Dorothy I. Height

grated schools, she experienced racial incidents that could have discouraged her. When she was a finalist in a state speech contest, the school principal and her Latin teacher drove her to Harrisburg to participate in the final. When they arrived at the hotel, they were not allowed in because the hotel did not welcome African-American guests. The teachers were shattered, but Dorothy was not going to let the incident bother her. She had brought her dress with her, and changed into it and entered the contest, which was being held elsewhere.

She was the last to speak, and her subject was Woodrow Wilson and the League of Nations. She ended her speech by saying that the message of peace had to be in the hearts of people. She won first prize from the panel of all white judges.

Dorothy graduated with honors and looked forward to going to college. Many students could not afford to go to college, but Dorothy had earned a $1,000 scholarship by winning an oratorical contest sponsored by the IBPOE (Independent Benevolent and Protective Order of Elks). And she had an older brother who was a doctor in New York. He planned to help pay her way through college.

Her dream was to go to Barnard College to study medicine. She knew it would take many years of preparation, but she wanted to help people. She took and passed the college entrance tests. She was thrilled when the dean of the school notified her that she was accepted.

Her parents were proud, and scraped together enough money for Dorothy's sister to travel with her to New York, but when they got to the campus Dorothy was told that the school had filled its quota of accepting only two black students. This news was devastating to Dorothy, since she had met all the requirements and had been informed that she was accepted. She was so disappointed she could not even talk about it for several days.

The brother who had planned to help her with expenses was in the hospital seriously ill with tuberculosis. He suggested that Dorothy try New York University. She did and was accepted and was able to use the scholarship from the Elks. Dorothy Height's brother died in the middle of her freshman year, and she decided to change her career plans. She would switch from medicine to social work, so that she could go to work sooner and start earning a living.

She took a heavy course load and went to school year around in order to make her scholarship go as far as possible. She earned her college degree in three years and her master's in one more year. She went to the New York School of Social Work for further study.

Dorothy Height began her professional career as a case worker for the New York City Welfare Department. This was a period of personal growth and soul-searching. She knew she wanted to help people live a good life, but was still trying to find the best way to do this.

Dorothy's aunt introduced her to the Reverend Adam Clayton Powell, Sr., pastor of the Abyssinian Baptist Church in Harlem. He had a tremendous influence on her thinking. As she said, "He liked to challenge us intellectually." During this time Dorothy was active in the Christian Youth Council and was selected to represent the United States at a conference in England. She came back to New York and quit her job at the

Welfare Department. She had decided her "life work must have a broader base."

She began a long career with the YWCA. While on the staff of the Harlem Y she met Mary McLeod Bethune. The date was November 7, 1937, and Mrs. Bethune was holding a meeting of the National Council of Negro Women, a national organization she had founded. She was to have a far-reaching impact on Dorothy Height's life.

Mrs. Bethune advised young people "to be part of something." She was a skillful organizer and pointed out that individuals and groups can increase their effectiveness by finding and working with other individuals and groups with similar goals. Dorothy later said, "I was inspired by Mrs. Bethune . . . to use whatever talent I had to be of some service to the community."

Following her meeting with Mrs. Bethune, Dorothy Height not only joined the National Council of Negro Women, she was actively involved in that organization during the many years she remained with and moved up to the executive level of the YWCA. Mary McLeod Bethune was impressed with Dorothy Height's dedication and became her mentor. Later, Dorothy followed in Mrs. Bethune's footsteps and became the national president of the National Council of Negro Women. There were twenty-five groups with a combined membership of four million when Dorothy Height became president in 1957. It has grown steadily ever since. For the nine years prior to assuming this leadership position, Dorothy Height served as national president of Delta Sigma Theta sorority.

Being an African-American woman, much of Dorothy

Dorothy Height cuts her 80th birthday cake.

Height's focus was on the African-American community and women's issues. But she realized that anything that affects African Americans and women affects the entire world population. Her goal was freedom, first-class citizenship, and participation for people everywhere. She worked to improve living, working, health, and educational conditions in the United States and elsewhere in the world.

Dorothy Height participated in major Civil Rights and human rights events in the 1950s and 1960s. She was the only woman on the United Council of Civil Rights Leaders. She worked closely with such leaders as Dr. Martin Luther King, Jr., Roy Wilkins, and A. Philip Randolph. In 1952, President John F. Kennedy appointed Dorothy Height as a member of the President's Commission on the Status of Women. In 1955, she served on the Council to the White House Conference "To Fulfill These Rights." She went to Israel on a mission of the Institute on Human Relations, and to Oxford, England, as a member of the Anglo-American Conference on Problems of Minority Integration. In 1972, she was a delegate to UNESCO's conference on "Woman and Her Rights" in Jamaica, and the following year she participated in the International Women's Year Conference of the UN in Mexico City. In 1980, she went to Copenhagen, Denmark, as official delegate for the United Nations Mid-Decade Conference on Women. In 1994, she participated in the Rainbow Coalition conference, and she was a speaker at the Million Man March in Washington in 1995 at the age of eighty-three.

In each of the capacities in which Dorothy Height served, she not only had ideas, she knew how to implement them.

Dorothy Height at a Black Family Reunion

Thinking of and successfully initiating the Black Family Reunion was only another example of her abilities. It was a way of continuing her efforts to help others. It is an event where participants can become better informed about how to improve the quality of their lives.

Dorothy Height's work has been recognized in many ways. She was inducted into the National Women's Hall of Fame, was awarded the Presidential Medal of Freedom (1994) and the Freedom Award presented by the National Civil Rights Museum. She also received the Spingarn Medal from the NAACP (National Association for the Advancement of Colored People).

She Didn't Take "No" for an Answer

CAST

Dorothy Height	A woman
Mother	First man
Nephew	A boy
First Narrator	Second man
Second Narrator	

Needed items: A bulletin board with announcements tacked to it at one side of the stage. A desk with several books and some papers on it at center stage. Paper cut into round shapes like coins. A rectangular piece of paper the size of a bank check.

SCENE 1

Dorothy is seated at the desk in the background as the two narrators speak to the audience.

FIRST NARRATOR: Dorothy Height's family lived in the town of Rankin, Pennsylvania, just outside Pittsburgh. She had always been a person who was able to size up a situation and act on it.

SECOND NARRATOR: For example, she never had a middle name—
or thought she needed one—until she was a senior in high
school. One day just before graduation, the teacher asked the
students how they wanted their names listed in the yearbook.

FIRST NARRATOR: Dorothy noticed that when other students were
called on, they all stated their first, last, and middle names. She
decided to do the same thing.

SECOND NARRATOR: Quickly she remembered an article she'd read
in that morning's newspaper about a young woman whose first
name was Dorothy and whose middle name was Irene. When
it was Dorothy's turn she said . . .

DOROTHY: Dorothy Irene Height . . .

SECOND NARRATOR: . . . as confidently as if she'd always had Irene
as a middle name!

FIRST NARRATOR: Dorothy wanted to continue her education after
high school, but America was in the midst of the Great Depression and money was in short supply. Dorothy knew that as
hardworking as her parents were, they could not afford to send
her to college.

(Dorothy leaves desk and goes over to look at the bulletin board.)

SECOND NARRATOR: She loved sports. Once when she was on her
way to a school basketball game, she noticed an announcement
on a bulletin board in the hall. It contained wonderful news.

FIRST NARRATOR: There was going to be an oratorical contest. Con-
testants would give speeches about the Constitution of the
United States. The first prize winner would receive a college
scholarship.

DOROTHY *(turning toward audience)*:   This is the opportunity I've been
wishing for! *(She copies the information on a piece of paper and walks
back to the desk.)*

FIRST NARRATOR: Dorothy studied hard to learn all she could about the Constitution of the United States, then she wrote an excellent speech.

DOROTHY *(looking at her paper)*:   This has got to be the best speech in the contest. *(She takes the books from the desk and walks off stage.)*

SECOND NARRATOR: Dorothy had to enter and win oratorical contests at the local, the state, the tri-state, and national levels in order to win the scholarship.

FIRST NARRATOR: She did win the local and state competitions. Next she was to compete in the tri-state contest where the Ohio, Pennsylvania, and West Virginia winners competed.

SCENE 2

Dorothy's mother and nephew are seated in the audience. Dorothy, a man, a woman, and a boy are standing over at one side of the stage quietly talking among themselves.

FIRST NARRATOR: When Dorothy and her mother and nephew arrived at the next place where she was to compete, she met an unexpected obstacle.

SECOND NARRATOR: A woman who was very active in the organization that was sponsoring the oratorical contest insisted that her hand-picked contestant represent the state of Pennsylvania instead of Dorothy. The man with her didn't speak up in Dorothy's behalf.

FIRST NARRATOR: Dorothy didn't like this one bit. It wasn't fair. She'd earned the right to participate in the contest and knew she wouldn't be able to go to college unless she could compete and win this round.

SECOND NARRATOR: She refused to be cheated out of her one chance.

FIRST NARRATOR: She sized up the situation. Quickly she walked over to her mother and said . . .

DOROTHY: Mama, may I have some money to make a long-distance telephone call?

SECOND NARRATOR: Now that was in the days when long-distance calls were made only in case of emergency. And those calls were almost always placed by adults. And here this high school girl was wanting to make a long-distance call.

NEPHEW: Dorothy, you're not old enough to make a long-distance telephone call.

DOROTHY: I have to make this call and try to straighten out a problem. That lady is trying to have that boy take my place in the contest.

MOTHER *(taking a handful of coins out of her purse)*:   Here you are, Dorothy. Good luck.

(Dorothy goes to an imaginary telephone that is across the stage from where she left the man, woman, and boy standing. She takes out a piece of paper, pretends to put money in the phone, and dials a number. She pretends to talk on the phone.)

DOROTHY: Hello, may I speak to Judge W. C. Houston? *(Pause)* Hello, Judge Houston. This is Dorothy Height and I need your help. I won the oratorical contest in Pennsylvania, and according to the rules I'm supposed to have a chance to compete at the tri-state meeting contest. But I'm at the tri-state meeting and a lady who's here says that she wants somebody else to compete instead of me. What must I do?

(Dorothy nods as she listens to what the person on the other end of the phone line says. At the end of the conversation, she says . . .)

DOROTHY: Thank you very much, Judge Houston. I'll tell them what you said.

(Dorothy goes over to where the man, woman, and boy are standing. She still has the piece of paper in her hand.)

DOROTHY: I just talked with Judge Houston and he said if I don't get a chance to compete, the contest will have to be held again. *(The woman acts surprised, as if she doesn't believe Dorothy.)*

FIRST MAN *(to woman)*:   If that is what Judge Houston said, we'll have to go along with it. I suggest you call the judge.

(The woman takes some coins out of her purse, then takes the paper out of Dorothy's hand and walks over to the telephone. She pretends to put the coins in the phone, and dials.)

WOMAN: Hello, is this Judge Houston's office? May I speak with him? Hello, Judge. I'm calling from the tri-state oratorical contest and I understand that a young lady named Dorothy Height just phoned you . . .

FIRST NARRATOR: Now it's the woman's turn to hear what the judge has to say. She listens, then says . . .

WOMAN: Yes, sir. All right. I'll do as you say. I'll withdraw my contestant.

(After she hangs up she goes back to where Dorothy, the man, and boy are standing. She pretends to be talking to the group, then she and the boy walk off stage. The man gestures to Dorothy to step up to the desk. Dorothy stands at the desk pretending to deliver a speech.)

SECOND NARRATOR: Dorothy Height not only took her rightful place in the regional contest, she won it.

FIRST NARRATOR: From there she had to go to the national contest in Chicago. There she had to compete against the winners of all the other regional contests in the United States.

SCENE 3

Dorothy and Mother walk across the stage rubbing their hands and acting like they're trying to get warm. They walk toward the second man, who is standing at one side of stage.

FIRST NARRATOR: Even though it was August, the weather was cold when Dorothy and her mother arrived in Chicago.

SECOND NARRATOR: Dorothy met with another obstacle when she went to get instructions for that final competition. She was told that she had to shorten her speech from its usual length of twenty minutes to just ten minutes. This was difficult because she had memorized her entire speech. It would be hard to shorten it and then memorize the new speech in time for that night's contest. *(Dorothy is seated at the desk, busily writing.)*

FIRST NARRATOR: . . . but she did it.

(Dorothy stands at desk. She pretends to say words and to gesture as if giving her speech. The second man, her mother, and nephew are seated in the audience.)

SECOND NARRATOR: Dorothy won the first prize and a scholarship to college.

(When Dorothy finishes speaking, they all clap. The second man rushes up to hand Dorothy a bank check and shake her hand. She smiles. Her mother and nephew rush up to hug her, and they all walk off the stage together.)

THURGOOD MARSHALL

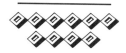

THE WORDS "Equal Justice Under Law" are chiseled in the marble above the entrance to the United States Supreme Court Building in Washington, D.C. Each year thousands of tourists and local residents read the famous motto.

Thurgood Marshall devoted his entire career—first as a lawyer and later as a Supreme Court justice—to making that motto apply to every American. His thorough knowledge of the United States Constitution made it possible for him to win rights for people who, up until that time, had been unable to enjoy the full rights of citizenship. His decisions made an impact on virtually every person and institution in America.

Throughout his long, productive career, Thurgood Marshall often had to work under unusual circumstances. But none were more unusual than the way he happened to learn the U.S. Constitution. Growing up, Thurgood Marshall was overly playful in school. He was always getting into mischief. His teacher would put him out of class for his behavior. Feeling that education should continue even if a student needed time out from class, she handed Thurgood Marshall a copy of the Constitution to study. She marked paragraphs for him to memorize. And she would quiz him before he returned to class.

Thurgood Marshall soon knew the Constitution by heart. He thought about the meaning of the document. When he saw that the Preamble began with "We the People of the United States . . ." he took it literally. He believed that those words should include *all* of the people, regardless of race, gender, or income. He realized that many Americans did not enjoy the civil rights of citizens. He was so successful in securing these rights that he earned the nickname of "Mr. Civil Rights."

He had firsthand knowledge of the need for everyone to be protected by the law. Thurgood Marshall was born on July 2, 1908, in Baltimore, and twelve years before his birth the Supreme Court had handed down an important decision in a case known as Plessy v. Ferguson that had a far-reaching impact on American life. The Court had ruled that it was all right for states to have "separate but equal" facilities for black and white citizens. In reality, the facilities provided for black citizens were seldom equal to those provided for white citizens.

Black Americans were treated like second-class citizens, in spite of the 13th, 14th, and 15th Amendments of the Constitution. They were denied the right to vote and to make full use of public institutions. Many tried to make the best of the situation. Thurgood Marshall's parents did. Although Baltimore, Maryland, had many racially segregated facilities, Mr. and Mrs. Marshall provided a stable home and a caring family. They lived at 1838 Druid Hill Avenue in a neighborhood with its own churches and businesses. They were respected members of the community.

Both of Thurgood's parents had a great influence on him. William Canfield Marshall earned a living first as a dining car waiter on a train, and later as a steward in an exclusive social club. He was an avid reader, an amateur writer, and he loved to debate.

Thurgood said his father turned him into a lawyer "by teaching me to argue, by challenging my logic on every point, by making me prove every statement I made." He and his father spent many happy hours in lively debate.

Norma Arica Marshall was a kindergarten teacher at the Henry Highland Garnet school that Thurgood and his older brother, Aubrey, attended. She took pride in the fact that the school was named for a black man whose education had made it possible for him to become an influential minister. She saw education as the one means by which black people could hope to make progress. She hoped that her younger son would decide to be a dentist when he grew up.

Although Thurgood Marshall was too young to decide on a career while in grade school, he did make a major decision. He decided to change his name. His parents had originally named him "Thouroughgood" after his father's father, who had taken that name when he enlisted in the Union Army. But young Thurgood found that name too long. He said, "By the time I reached second grade, I got tired of spelling that all out and had it shortened to 'Thurgood.'" This was one of the first of many decisions he would make.

Even with the warmth and sense of security given by his family, Thurgood Marshall had some unhappy experiences as a result of the "separate but equal" law. Sometimes no facilities for blacks were available. One time when he was in downtown Baltimore he felt the need to use the bathroom, but there were no restrooms that black people could use. He attempted to solve the problem by hopping on a streetcar and rushing home, but made it only as far as the front door. He never forgot that humiliating moment.

As a teenager, he had a part-time job as delivery boy for a hat shop. Once, during the busy Easter season, he had more than the usual number of hats to deliver. He was carrying such a tall stack of big, round hatboxes that he could not see over them. Without realizing it, he pushed in front of a white woman to get on the streetcar. A man who saw this spoke to Thurgood in such a mean way that he put the hatboxes down and balled up his fists, ready to fight. He didn't have many fights, however. For one thing, he realized he could not fight everyone who gave him a reason to be angry. The other thing was his size. Very few people would pick a fight with a young man who stood six feet two inches tall and weighed 210 pounds.

Thurgood Marshall attended Frederick Douglass High School in Baltimore. He was full of mischief and liked to argue. It was his mischief-making that got him sent out of class to study the Constitution. His interest in arguing and debating was channeled in another way. Their class had a Class Court in which they discussed student concerns and problems. Thurgood Marshall took charge of it. At that point in his life he had no plans to become a lawyer, but he left high school with the foundation for his future career.

Thurgood Marshall entered college in September of 1925. His mother still hoped he would become a dentist, and had sold her engagement ring to make it possible for him to attend Lin-

Supreme Court Justice Thurgood Marshall

coln University in Pennsylvania. Lincoln had been known for academic excellence since it opened in 1854. The members of its all-white faculty were well educated and conscientious. Most members of its student body of young black men felt destined to accomplish something in their lives. Many did. Poet Langston Hughes, entertainer Cab Calloway, and Nnamdi Azikiwe, who became president of Nigeria, were Thurgood Marshall's classmates.

Thurgood was more interested in having a good time than in studying dentistry. During his sophomore year, he was put out of school for practical jokes he played on some freshmen students. This experience made him realize that it was time to settle down. As he put it, "I got the horsin' around out of my system." He returned to Lincoln with a more serious attitude and graduated in June of 1930. One of the things he liked best was the debating, and he did it very well. He started thinking of law as a field he would like better than dentistry.

The college campus, like Marshall's home, provided a setting in which each person was respected. However, the "separate but equal" law applied to life outside the campus. The movie theater in the town of Oxford required black persons to sit in the balcony. One night Langston Hughes and other classmates of Thurgood Marshall's set out to change this. They bought their tickets, but instead of going to the balcony, they sat on the first floor. An usher asked them to move, but they remained seated. They felt they had paid their money and should be able to choose where they wanted to sit—just like other patrons. The students' action resulted in a change at the theater. From that night on, students could sit wherever they wished.

The students not only desegregated the movie theater, they also voted to integrate the faculty of Lincoln University. Graduates of Lincoln and other black schools would have the opportunity to join white faculty members in continuing Lincoln's tradition of excellence in education.

Thurgood Marshall was still in college when he met his wife-to-be. He and Vivian Burey met at a church dance and were married at the beginning of his senior year. He worked at odd jobs to pay for the double responsibilities of maintaining a home and paying college expenses.

Vivian—or "Buster," as he called her—encouraged her husband in his studies. She was the stabilizing force he needed in his life. Thurgood wanted to study law and applied to the University of Maryland, but it denied him admission. It did not maintain a separate law school for African-American students and refused to integrate the one it maintained for white students. Marshall applied to and was accepted by the law school at the all-black Howard University in Washington, D.C. Each day he commuted the 90 miles to and from his parents' home. This meant getting up at 5:00 A.M. each morning after having worked an evening job to help pay tuition. He spent afternoons studying at the library.

Howard University got its first black president, Dr. Mordecai Johnson, just a short while before Thurgood Marshall enrolled. Charles Hamilton Houston headed the law school. Houston had studied law at Harvard and the University of Madrid in Spain. He felt it was essential that segregation be brought to an end, both for the sake of African Americans and the country as a whole. He believed the lawyers he was training would be the ones to bring about this change. He prepared them by making sure they had a thorough knowledge of the Constitution. Charles Houston and Thurgood Marshall soon earned each other's respect.

Houston's efforts coincided with those of the National Association for the Advancement of Colored People (NAACP) to hasten the end of segregation. He and others felt that the Plessy v. Ferguson decision could be overturned. The place to start was the schools.

Houston trained his students in mock, or pretend, trials. He and other lawyers would make legal arguments just as they would have presented them in an actual courtroom. The students were to challenge these arguments. These mock trials sharpened the students' skills and gave them valuable experience in courtroom procedure.

Marshall was inspired. He later said, "I heard law books were to dig into, so I dug, way deep. I got through simply by overwhelming the job." He spent long hours carefully preparing his arguments. He had a talent for expressing complex ideas in thoughtful, simple language. He graduated from Howard University at the top of his class.

He began his law career by opening a small office in Baltimore in 1933. That was in the midst of the Great Depression. People came to him with their legal problems, but few had money to pay him. He seldom had money to buy lunch. He would bring sandwiches from home, one for his secretary and one for himself.

Marshall was also legal counsel for the Baltimore branch of the NAACP. He participated in a variety of cases. He took part in cases to have the Maryland board of education pay equal salaries to its teachers. (White teachers had been paid twice as much as black teachers.) But the case which especially appealed to him was one which challenged the University of Maryland's practice of denying admission to black applicants. Donald Gaines Murray's situation was much like Marshall's had been a few years earlier. To the delight of many, Thurgood Marshall won the Murray case in the Maryland Court of Appeals. No American court had ever ordered an educational institution to admit a black student. Eventually, Marshall would go before the U.S. Supreme Court and win 29 of 32 cases, but no victory was sweeter than this one.

Shortly after, Marshall was tapped by his old law professor, Charles Houston, to become assistant special counsel for the national NAACP. The two spent most of 1936 traveling throughout the South gathering information that would help them in the fight against school segregation. Marshall's car served as their office. They stayed at friends' homes, since there were no black hotels and white hotels were closed to them.

In 1938, Houston resigned as the NAACP's chief legal counsel, and Marshall took his place. He argued cases in many small Southern towns, and continued gathering information about school desegregation. The rights he sought to protect ranged from voting and serving on juries to owning property and traveling from state to state without being segregated. He fearlessly challenged local practices.

His courage and accomplishments did not go unnoticed. In 1946, he received the Spingarn Medal, the NAACP's highest honor. In 1950, he was appointed Director-Counsel for the NAACP Legal Defense and Educational Fund, Inc.

Marshall's interest in school desegregation remained strong. Lawsuits in a number of cities had been unsuccessful in the local and state courts, so he and other lawyers working with him planned a strategy. They combined all the school cases under the title Brown v. Board of Education of Topeka (Kansas) and asked the U.S. Supreme Court to make a ruling.

On December 9, 1952, the day of opening arguments, the courtroom was packed and people were lined up outdoors. Marshall's opposition was John W. Davis, one of the most experienced lawyers in the United States. Each had three days to present arguments.

Thurgood Marshall had been waiting for this opportunity for many years. He and his staff made thorough preparation. Nothing must be overlooked. Too much was at stake. The three days of arguments ended in what appeared to be a tie. The justices wanted more information and presented a list of questions. Then Chief Justice Fred Vinson died suddenly. A year after they first argued the case, attorneys Marshall and Davis presented answers to those questions.

The Supreme Court did not hand down its decision for seventeen long months. Then, on May 17, 1954, Chief Justice Earl Warren read the court's unanimous decision that in the field of public education "separate but equal" had no place.

A year and a half after that decision, Mrs. Rosa Parks made her courageous decision about where she would sit on a bus. Thurgood Marshall and the NAACP took the issue of bus segregation to the Supreme Court. The court ruled that bus segregation was unconstitutional also.

In 1961, President John F. Kennedy nominated Thurgood

Thurgood Marshall (fourth from right) and other lawyers who successfully argued the Brown v. Board of Education case.

Marshall to be a judge on the U.S. Court of Appeals in New York. His wife, "Buster," did not live to see him in this new role. She had died of cancer not long after his victory in the Brown case. His second wife, Cecilia S. Suyat, and their two sons, Thurgood, Jr., and John, looked on with pride as Thurgood, Sr., was sworn in as judge.

Four years later, President Lyndon B. Johnson asked Marshall to be Solicitor General of the United States. He would decide which cases the government would appeal to the Supreme Court and then argue those cases. In 1967, President

Johnson appointed Marshall to be Associate Justice of the U.S. Supreme Court. The Senate had to approve the appointment and there were some senators who objected. But Johnson replied that Thurgood Marshall was ". . . the right man" and appointing him to the court was ". . . the right thing to do."

Being selected as one of the nine justices was a tribute to Marshall's accomplishments. Prior to that time there had never been an African-American justice on the court, although many of its decisions affected the lives of African Americans. Now the court would benefit from the insights of a man who had personally experienced the "separate but equal" doctrine, the man who had done so much to overturn that doctrine.

Thurgood Marshall's legal career spanned fifty-eight years. During that time he had seen and made many changes in American society. On June 27, 1991—a few days before his eighty-second birthday—he announced his retirement from the Supreme Court. When reporters asked him how he would sum up his long and distinguished career, he answered, "I did what I could with what I had."

Tributes to his life and work were made in many ways. He received the $100,000 Liberty Award at a Fourth of July ceremony at Independence Hall in Philadelphia. The University of Maryland—which had refused to admit him years earlier—named its law library for him. The city of Baltimore placed a larger-than-life statue of him outside the Federal Court House. The law school at Texas Southern University was named for him. The Thurgood Marshall Scholarship helps make it possible for students to attend thirty-six black colleges and universities.

Thurgood Marshall died on January 24, 1993. As his body lay in state at the Supreme Court, so many people came, wishing to show their respect, that the line stretched for three blocks. When Chief Justice William Rehnquist eulogized Thurgood Marshall at his funeral in the National Cathedral, he referred to the words "Equal Justice Under Law" inscribed above the entrance to the Supreme Court. "No one individual did more to make these words a reality than Thurgood Marshall."

Marshall was buried in a private ceremony at Arlington National Cemetery. He had devoted his life attempting to assure equal justice under the law for all American citizens.

The Case of the Dirty Sweatshirt

C A S T

Judge	Defendant
Bailiff	First Narrator
Plaintiff	Second Narrator

The Plaintiff is the person who files a complaint. The Defendant is the person against whom the complaint is filed. The Bailiff is an officer of the court.

FIRST NARRATOR: Mrs. Ivora Gibson attended Frederick Douglass High School in Baltimore with Thurgood Marshall. In their classroom there were occasional disputes. Their teacher decided to hold a mock court.

SECOND NARRATOR: A mock court is a pretend court. Law students use them to practice presenting cases in court. The teacher thought it would be a good way for students to resolve the kinds of problems that came up in school.

FIRST NARRATOR: The teacher knew that Thurgood Marshall had memorized the U.S. Constitution. She selected him to be the judge for the mock court.

SECOND NARRATOR: Since we weren't at Frederick Douglass High School with Ivora Gibson and Thurgood Marshall, we can only guess at what cases were brought before the classroom court. This one might have happened. It is about two students who have hall lockers next to each other.

BAILIFF: Hear ye! Hear ye! The classroom court is now in session. Judge Marshall is presiding. Please rise. (*Everyone in the courtroom stands until the Judge enters and is seated.*)

JUDGE: This is the Case of the Dirty Sweatshirt. I have read the complaint.

FIRST NARRATOR: The Plaintiff claims that he loaned a sweatshirt to the Defendant and that the sweatshirt was dirty when the Defendant returned it. The Plaintiff is demanding compensation.

SECOND NARRATOR: Compensation means payment. The Defendant plans to show that there was a good reason for the sweatshirt not being returned in the condition in which he received it.

JUDGE (*speaking to Plaintiff*): Please tell the Court how you happened to loan your sweatshirt to the Defendant.

PLAINTIFF: I was trying to be nice. It was sunny and warm in the morning, but then the temperature dropped about 20 degrees by time to go home. So I loaned the Defendant my sweatshirt. He was cold.

JUDGE: What did you wear to keep yourself warm?

PLAINTIFF: I wore my heavy jacket.

JUDGE: How did you happen to have both a jacket and sweatshirt at school?

PLAINTIFF: I hadn't cleaned out my locker since winter. My jacket was in there from a day when it warmed up while we were in school. The sweatshirt was from gym class.

JUDGE: Did you say you wanted the sweatshirt back the next day and in the same condition as when you loaned it?

PLAINTIFF: I asked him to bring it back the next day.

JUDGE (*speaking to Defendant*): Is that correct? Did the Plaintiff say he wanted the sweatshirt back the next day and in the same condition it was in when he gave it to you?

DEFENDANT: He said, 'Bring it back tomorrow.' He didn't say anything about what condition it should be in.

JUDGE: What condition was the sweatshirt in when you received it?

DEFENDANT: It was wrinkled and smelly from gym class, but I didn't care, as long as it was warm.

JUDGE: Did you return the sweatshirt the next day and in the same condition in which you received it?

DEFENDANT: I returned it the next day, but as I was getting on the bus I accidentally brushed up against the outside of the bus and some dirt got on the sweatshirt.

JUDGE: Did you try to get the dirt off?

DEFENDANT: I thought about washing it, but in order to get it dry in time to return it the next day I would have had to put it in a hot dryer. I was afraid it would shrink.

FIRST NARATOR (*as Judge leaves the room*): The Judge takes a brief recess to consider his decision.

SECOND NARRATOR *(as Judge returns to his seat)*: The Judge soon returns and announces his decision. Let's hear what the Judge ruled.

JUDGE: I rule for the Defendant who was loaned the sweatshirt. He did return it on the following day. The Plaintiff did not request that the sweatshirt be returned in the same condition in which it was received. The Defendant admits that there was dirt from the bus on it, but he was protective in not wanting to take a chance on the sweatshirt shrinking if he washed it. No compensation is justified.

FIRST NARRATOR: This was only an imaginary court case in school. Thurgood Marshall went on to become one of the outstanding justices of the United States Supreme Court.

Mary Ann Shadd

IN THE MIDDLE OF THE NIGHT young Mary Ann Shadd heard a muffled knock at the door, followed by a whispered welcome, "Come in." It was not unusual for her to wake up and hear her parents inviting strangers into the house. Her parents were free black people who risked their own freedom by using their home as an Underground Railroad station, or stopping place, for people escaping from slavery. These acts of courage made a lasting impression on Mary Ann Shadd.

When she grew up, she followed her parents' example in that she risked serious consequences for doing what she believed to be right. She overcame powerful obstacles to operate a school in Canada, to become North America's first black woman newspaper editor, and to earn her law degree at the age of sixty-one. She was so unafraid to tackle challenges that her family affectionately called her "the Rebel."

Mary Ann Shadd was born on October 9, 1823, in Wilmington, Delaware, the oldest of thirteen children. Not much is known about her mother, Harriett Parnell Shadd, except that she was born in North Carolina in 1806. More is known about her father, Abraham Doras Shadd.

Abraham Shadd was born in Delaware in 1801. His mother was originally from Santo Domingo and his father was the son of a German soldier in General Braddock's command. Abraham was a shoemaker with a thriving business. He inherited some property and purchased more. He was a free man and well-to-do, and he strongly opposed slavery.

All during Mary Ann's formative years, her father was an ardent abolitionist. From the time she was seven until she was ten, her father was the Delaware representative at the National Convention for the Improvement of Free People in the United States. He eventually became president of that group, and was one of the founders of the American Anti-Slavery Society. He became a well-known spokesman for the abolition movement.

Abraham Shadd was an agent for the *Liberator* newspaper, one of the most controversial antislavery papers. It was published by Bostonian William Lloyd Garrison. Shadd's views were just as uncompromising as those of the paper. He believed that abolition of slavery was only a first step. He also emphasized the need for education, thrift, and hard work.

The Shadd family was in the position of being free black people in the slave state of Delaware. Mary Ann was most affected because Delaware did not provide schools for black children. Education was so important to Abraham and Harriett Shadd that they left family, friends, and property in Delaware so that their children could attend school in Pennsylvania. When Mary Ann was ten, they moved to West Chester and her parents enrolled her in a school operated by Quakers. She completed her studies and returned to Wilmington as a teacher. (At that time it was not necessary for teachers to com-

Mary Ann Shadd

plete college.) Later she taught in West Chester and Norristown, Pennsylvania; Trenton, New Jersey; and New York City.

Some abolitionists had encouraged free black people to migrate to Canada in the belief that they could enjoy the same rights as any other immigrants. There wasn't a pressing need to leave the United States, however, for many freedmen and fugitives had found in the northern states some safe places to live and work. That security disappeared when the U.S. Congress passed the 1850 Fugitive Slave Act.

The Act allowed slave catchers to go into northern states and force any black person into slavery. It did not require the slave catchers to prove that a person was actually an escaped slave. The law prompted an exodus. Thousands of African Americans headed for Canada.

Mary Ann Shadd was teaching in Norristown, Pennsylvania, when the Fugitive Slave Act was passed. She knew that people making the move northward were setting out for unknown territory. In 1851 she went to Toronto, Canada, to a convention where a number of concerned black people were meeting to discuss immigration. She stayed on in Canada to investigate the possibilities of settlement there.

There was an urgent need for teachers, for the newly arrived immigrants were eager to get an education that had been denied them as slaves. Mary Ann began teaching at a school in Windsor, a city right across the river from Detroit, Michigan. She had gone to Windsor at the suggestion of Henry and Mary Bibb.

Henry Bibb was a former slave who had come to Canada six years earlier. He was a founding member of the Refugee Home

Society. He and his wife edited a newspaper called *Voice of the Fugitive*, and they operated a school in Sandwich, a town near Windsor.

Originally, Mary Ann Shadd had a lot of respect for the Bibbs, but her views soon changed. Almost immediately she and the Bibbs had a difference of opinion about how she should operate her school. She needed funding for the school and had been told that the American Missionary Association was thinking of hiring teachers to work in Canada. She wrote, hoping that the Association would fund her school, but didn't get an answer for months. Finally, they agreed to pay $125 a year—half the amount she had requested. Somehow she made do and not only taught her students basic reading and writing but the lessons she'd learned from her father—thrift and hard work. She wanted them to become self-sufficient Canadian citizens as quickly as possible. The Bibbs seemed to treat them as dependent refugees.

Working with former slaves, Mary Ann became convinced that a "what to expect in Canada" guidebook would be helpful. She prepared a 44-page booklet and called it *A Plea for Emigration*. However, it was more often referred to by its subtitle, *Notes of Canada West*. She packed its pages with details about climate, election laws, money, business and educational opportunities, geography, and crops. She sold the booklet for 12½ cents, so that she would be able to pay the printer. Her choice of printer caused another disagreement with the Bibbs.

Back in Pennsylvania, Abraham Shadd was considering moving with his family and other friends to Canada. He visited his daughter in 1852. Meanwhile, Mary Ann lost her respect for Henry and Mary Bibb because of the way they operated the Refugee Home Society. She felt that they misrepresented the conditions of the refugees in Canada in their newspaper. When she complained, the Bibbs ran an article revealing that the American Missionary Society was funding her school, and as a result that funding was stopped. Mary Ann knew she would have to close her school.

Since childhood, Mary Ann Shadd had been aware of the power of the press. A teacher once told her " . . . the printed and the spoken word is never lost." She had just seen the Bibbs use their newspaper to destroy her school. She began to think of establishing a newspaper in which she could express her own views.

About this time a man named Samuel Ringgold Ward arrived in Canada. He had experience writing for a number of antislavery newspapers, and Mary Ann got Ward interested in her idea of establishing a newspaper. They would call it *The Provincial Freeman*. Ward had the title of editor.

That title was in name only. Ward was considered by many to be as excellent a speaker as Frederick Douglass and he traveled extensively making speeches. From the beginning, the plan was for Mary Ann Shadd to be the real editor, but she realized that very few women even wrote for newspapers. She knew the paper would be more readily accepted if readers identified it with a highly respected male journalist.

The first edition of *The Provincial Freeman* was published in March, 1853. It included a variety of features: articles for and against the Refugee Home Society, local news, a poem about the invention of the telegraph. The primary purpose was to inform readers of the progress black people were making in Canada. The newspaper's motto was "Self-Reliance Is the Road to Independence."

After the first edition of the newspaper was published, Mary Ann went to Philadelphia where she gave a series of lectures to encourage more people to emigrate to Canada. She spent most of the next year lecturing and her tour was a success. She got enough support for her newspaper to continue publishing it. When she returned to Canada, she moved the offices of *The Provincial Freeman* to Toronto, a bustling port city with a number of prosperous black businessmen interested in the paper.

Initially, Mary Ann Shadd listed her name in the paper as "M. A. Shadd, Publishing Agent." Since most readers didn't know that M. A. stood for Mary Ann, most letters were addressed to "Mr. Shadd" or "Mr. Freeman." In the summer of 1854, her sister, Amelia, began to help edit the newspaper. It was then that Mary Ann Shadd revealed her real name and that her sister was on the staff. From then on she was addressed as "the editress."

Amelia was soon able to take care of the day-to-day operations of the paper, and Mary Ann turned to other things. She formed an organization called the Provincial Union to support the black newspapers in Canada. Her plan was to get prominent citizens in different cities to be representatives for the newspapers in order to reach new subscribers. Again, she set out on a lecture tour.

She returned to Toronto in February of 1855, and resumed her work as editor. When Amelia left to be married, their brother Isaac joined the staff. By June of that year there was so much public outrage at the fact that *The Provincial Freeman* was edited by a woman, the paper was in danger of being put out of business. This was disheartening, but Mary Ann informed her readers that the newspaper would soon have a new editor—a man named the Reverend William P. Newman. She moved the offices from Toronto to Chatham, and ended her final editorial with a bit of advice: "To colored women, we have a word—we have broken the editorial ice . . . so go to Editing, as many of you as are willing and able . . ." She also asked readers to support the paper by subscribing.

Her parents had settled about twelve miles from Chatham in the highly successful black community of Buxton, which had been established by a Scotsman named the Reverend William King. He had married the daughter of a plantation owner in Louisiana and after his wife's death he was the owner of fifteen slaves. He decided to free them and take them to Canada where they would be the nucleus of a new settlement. He was convinced that if black people had the same economic and educational opportunities as anyone else, they could successfully create a self-supporting community.

Within a few years the Buxton Settlement was flourishing. The school was the pride of the community. Some slave owners claimed that black people could not learn, but the Buxton school proved them wrong. Six years after it opened, six young black men were ready for college. One of them, James T. Rapier, became a U.S. Congressman.

Black settlers weren't the only ones who recognized the high quality of education the Buxton school provided. White settlers in the area asked to have their children go to the school, too.

Canada was in a depression in the 1850s. All kinds of businesses were affected. *The Provincial Freeman* was no exception. The paper needed funds to continue publication, so Mary Ann Shadd went traveling again. In Philadelphia, she made such an effective speech that she changed Frederick Douglass' attitude toward emigration. He wrote in his newspaper, "She suc-

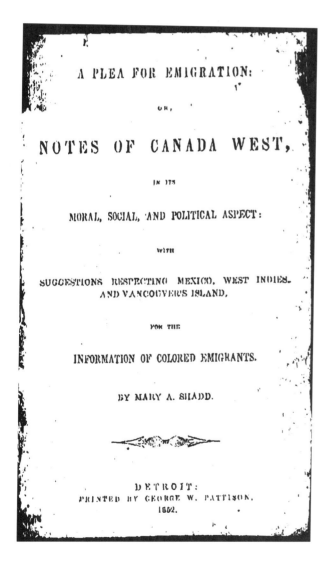

A PLEA FOR EMIGRATION:

OR,

NOTES OF CANADA WEST,

IN ITS

MORAL, SOCIAL, AND POLITICAL ASPECT:

WITH

SUGGESTIONS RESPECTING MEXICO, WEST INDIES,
AND VANCOUVER'S ISLAND,

FOR THE

INFORMATION OF COLORED EMIGRANTS.

BY MARY A. SHADD.

DETROIT:
PRINTED BY GEORGE W. PATTISON,
1852.

Title page for
Notes of Canada West,
published by
Mary Ann Shadd.

ceeded in making one of the most convincing and telling speeches in favor of Canadian emigration I ever heard . . ." She also debated and unanimously defeated a man who opposed emigration. But her triumph was the benefit held in her honor. A large interracial audience gathered in a Philadelphia hall to pay tribute to her as founder and editor of a newspaper. The highlight of the evening was a recital by Elizabeth Taylor Greenfield, an internationally famous soprano known as the "Black Swan." Miss Greenfield did not accept payment, so that all the money could go to Mary Ann Shadd.

Wedding bells rang for Mary Ann Shadd on January 3, 1856. She was thirty-two years old when she married Thomas F. Cary. He had been supportive of her activities related to *The Provincial Freeman*. He and two brothers were barbers in Toronto, and he had three children by a former marriage.

Almost immediately Mary Ann left on another fund-raising trip. Times were difficult for her newspaper. Poor health forced the Reverend Newman to resign as editor. Her brother Isaac got some printing contracts from the town of Chatham, but even the town was unable to pay promptly.

In 1858, when John Brown was planning his raid on Harper's Ferry, he met with a number of leaders in Chatham. Thomas Cary and Isaac Shadd were among them, and Brown stayed at Isaac's home.

In August of 1857, the Carys' daughter, Sarah Elizabeth, was born. Three years later their son, Linton, was born. Thomas Cary died on November 29, 1860, and Mary Ann was left a widow with two small children to raise and educate.

The American Civil War began in 1861. African Americans

on both sides of the Canadian border were eager to work for the Union forces. Mary Ann wanted to support the war effort, and she accepted an offer to become an army recruiting officer. She saw this as a chance to do useful work and have a regular income.

When the war ended, Mary Ann Shadd Cary recognized the great desire the newly freed slaves had for education. For a time she taught in Detroit, Michigan. In 1869, she moved to Washington, D.C., where she continued to write and teach. She became a regular contributor to two locally published papers, and was a school principal for seventeen years. In addition, she managed to continue her fund-raising trips for the newspapers.

At night she studied law at Howard University. She encountered some delays in receiving her degree and being admitted to the bar of the Supreme Court of the District of Columbia. But she graduated in 1883 and resigned from her career as an educator to begin practicing law. Now she had a new means of working for racial equality and women's rights.

The Fifteenth Amendment to the U.S. Constitution extended the right to vote to black men, but excluded all women. In 1880, Mary Ann started the Colored Women's Progressive Franchise Association. Her goals included working for equal rights, establishing a newspaper, supporting black businesses, and opening up professions to women.

By this time her children were young adults. Sarah Elizabeth had studied at Howard University and was married. Linton was a messenger at the House of Representatives. He died in 1892.

Despite serious health problems, Mary Ann continued to write and lecture as long as she could. She had once said, "It is better to wear out than to rust out." She died on June 5, 1893.

In her lifetime, Mary Ann Shadd Cary demonstrated courage. She stood up for her beliefs and risked serious consequences for doing what she believed to be right. She influenced and inspired many people in both the United States and Canada.

A Memorable Visit

CAST

First Narrator
Second Narrator
Mary Ann Shadd Cary

Isaac Shadd, Mary Ann's brother
Garrison Shadd, another brother
Alfred Shadd, Garrison's son

FIRST NARRATOR: Once Mary Ann Shadd Cary moved to Washington, D.C., she seldom got back to Canada. However, she did make at least one trip in the late 1880s.

SECOND NARRATOR: That's the trip during which she met—and made a great impression on—a young nephew of hers.

FIRST NARRATOR: His name was Alfred Schmitz Shadd. He was a teenaged son of Mary Ann's brother Garrison, who had become a wealthy farmer.

SECOND NARRATOR: Alfred lived with his parents near Chatham, Ontario, the town where Mary Ann had published *The Provincial Freeman*, the first newspaper in North America to be edited by a black woman.

SCENE 1

FIRST NARRATOR: It is likely that Mary Ann met her nephew at a family gathering at Isaac's house in Chatham.

SECOND NARRATOR: A horse-drawn carriage stops at the front door.

ISAAC SHADD (*going to the door*):   Well, Mary Ann, you are about to meet the young man I've been telling you about.

MARY ANN: I'm looking forward to it.

FIRST NARRATOR: Garrison and Alfred come in.

SECOND NARRATOR: Isaac and Mary Ann greet them.

GARRISON SHADD: Mary Ann, let me introduce my son, Alfred.

FIRST NARRATOR: After the introduction, Garrison goes across the room to visit with Isaac, as Mary Ann and Alfred get acquainted.

MARY ANN: Hello, Alfred.

ALFRED: Hello, Aunt Mary. I've been hearing about you for as long as I can remember—about your teaching and writing and becoming a lawyer.

MARY ANN: Are you interested in any of those things?

ALFRED: Yes, actually I'd like to combine a number of careers—just as you did. I'm interested in teaching and writing. Instead of going into law, though, I plan to study medicine and may go into politics like Grandpa Abraham Shadd.

MARY ANN: By all means do! There's nothing you can't accomplish if you try. I won't tell you it's easy, but I will tell you it is well worth the effort.

ALFRED: I am so glad to hear you say that. I may sound overly ambitious to try to do so many things. But I'm interested in a lot of things and feel that they are all connected.

MARY ANN: That's true. Don't let anything discourage you. You have to believe in yourself. I once heard an elderly man say, "To think you can, gives you the will that can."

ALFRED: I like that saying. My father told me that you used to be a school principal by day, a law student at night, and a parent, writer, and speaker in-between times.

MARY ANN *(laughing)*:   Yes, I did do all those things. Sometimes I look back and wonder how, but I did it and I'm glad. You will be, too. Where do you plan to study medicine?

ALFRED: The University of Toronto.

MARY ANN: That's a fine school. Toronto's a nice city, too. My husband was from Toronto, and I published *The Provincial Freeman* there before we moved to Chatham. Your Aunt Amelia helped me edit the paper in Toronto. After she left to get married, I moved the *Freeman* offices to Chatham and your Uncle Isaac and I were both editors.

ALFRED: I hadn't realized all that. I did know you managed to keep that paper going through some tough times.

MARY ANN: Yes, but writing for a newspaper made it possible for me to meet so many people and do so many things!

ALFRED: Like what?

MARY ANN: Well, you've heard of John Brown, haven't you?

ALFRED: Yes, he led that famous raid on Harper's Ferry.

MARY ANN: Well, he came to Chatham in the spring of 1858 and he stayed right here—in your Uncle Isaac's house—during the Chatham Convention when he and his friends were working on his provisional constitution and making plans for the raid.

ALFRED: Really? John Brown stayed in *this* house?

MARY ANN: Yes, he did.

ALFRED: I've heard so many different opinions about him. What was he really like?

MARY ANN: He was a very thoughtful and caring man. He had a compelling presence, with his straight posture and his long flowing beard.

ALFRED: The man you saw doesn't sound like the wild-eyed rebel that some people think he was.

MARY ANN: He was a very dedicated man and he did some very daring things. The raid on Harper's Ferry is the best example.

ALFRED: Why did John Brown come to Chatham?

MARY ANN: He wanted to help bring an end to slavery, but he wasn't satisfied to stop at that. He held a political convention here to work out a democratic government for the slave-free society he hoped for.

ALFRED: Did any of our family members take part in the convention?

MARY ANN: Yes. They not only took part in planning the constitution, they were selected to be officers in the new organization. At the time of the raid, my husband, Thomas Cary, was chairman of John Brown's provisional government and your Uncle Isaac was secretary.

ALFRED: What about the raid? Did any of our family join John Brown's army?

MARY ANN: None of our family members did, but a young man who used to live here at Uncle Isaac's house went. His name was Osborn Anderson. He was one of the few survivors.

ALFRED: Did he ever tell about his experience?

MARY ANN: Yes, I helped him write a pamphlet called "A Voice from Harper's Ferry." Uncle Isaac probably has a copy.

GARRISON SHADD *(walking over to Mary Ann and Alfred)*: I see the two of you have a lot to talk about. I'm sorry to disrupt your conversation, but Alfred and I need to leave now if we're going to get home in time to do our evening chores around the farm.

ALFRED *(to Mary Ann)*: Aunt Mary, I have really enjoyed talking with you. I liked hearing about John Brown, but I also want to thank you for encouraging me to try all the things I want to do with my life.

MARY ANN *(to Alfred as she and her brother Isaac walk to the door with their guests)*: You're welcome. I've enjoyed talking with you, too. I'm getting up in years, and am so glad to know I have a nephew who will carry on some of the work I've started.

ALFRED *(as he hugs Mary Ann)*: Good-bye. I'll try hard to make you proud.

SCENE 2

FIRST NARRATOR: Alfred Shadd's first career was as a teacher in his hometown. He was still quite young when he began teaching.

He wasn't much older than many of his students, some of whom were his cousins.

SECOND NARRATOR: He used to have fun racing his students to school, then ringing the bell and telling them they were late. They all had a good laugh and then started their studies.

FIRST NARRATOR: After teaching several years, Alfred became a student at the University of Toronto. He finished medical school in 1898.

SECOND NARRATOR: He moved to the Province of Saskatchewan where he distinguished himself as a doctor . . .

FIRST NARRATOR: . . . for people *and* for animals. His schooling was in human medicine, but having grown up on a farm, he knew how to care for animals.

SECOND NARRATOR: "Doc Shadd" was the only black person and the only doctor in the Province.

FIRST NARRATOR: He was also the newspaper editor, a scientist, a rancher, and a politician.

SECOND NARRATOR: His Aunt Mary would have been very proud.

A. G. GASTON

Dr. A. G. Gaston had more money than some banks. At one point he was reportedly worth $140 million. He didn't think of that as an especially remarkable accomplishment, however. "What I have done anybody can do . . ." If asked how, he would answer, "Find a need and fill it."

That's exactly what he did—over and over again—throughout his long productive career. From grade school days, A. G. Gaston had the ability to recognize what services people wanted—then he opened a business to supply those needs.

Born on July 4, 1892, Arthur George Gaston was still going to work daily and making effective business decisions when he celebrated his 100th birthday on July 4, 1992. The city of Birmingham, Alabama—the center of Gaston's business empire—celebrated. Mayor Richard Arrington declared the day "A. G. Gaston Day." There were parades. Local and national radio, television, and newspapers featured this remarkable man. And there were fireworks, of course.

A. G. Gaston had conceived and successfully operated ten businesses, employing hundreds of people. They ranged from the Booker T. Washington Insurance Company, the foundation of his operations, to radio stations WENN-FM and WAGG-AM. He was a man who cared about the people who had helped make him successful. He prided himself on having selected capable and dedicated workers. At age ninety-five, he transferred the ownership of his businesses to his 400 employees.

He encouraged all people of voting age to exercise their rights of citizenship by registering and voting in local and national elections. He was a founding member of Birmingham's Community Affairs Committee and played a key role in the Civil Rights Movement. He posted $5,000 bail to free Dr. Martin Luther King, Jr., after Dr. King wrote his famous "Letter from a Birmingham City Jail." A. G. Gaston also allowed Dr. King and other Civil Rights workers to use land he owned as overnight campsites when they marched across the state of Alabama. At other times he acted as a go-between between the black and white communities.

Believing that young people are the future, he attempted to see that they had a good start in life. He sponsored scholarships throughout the Alabama college system, especially encouraging young law students. He established the A. G. Gaston Boys' and Girls' Club to provide wholesome recreation for young students.

Through the years, institutions and organizations honored A. G. Gaston for his achievements and contributions. Many asked him to serve on their boards of directors. Universities awarded him honorary degrees, giving him the title of Dr. A. G. Gaston.

Arthur George Gaston was born in a log cabin in the small

town of Demopolis, Alabama. His grandparents, Joe and Idella Gaston, were former slaves who had bought a plot of fertile farm land. His parents lived with his grandparents until his father got a job on the railroad. After his father died, his mother worked as a cook in the home of a wealthy family in North Carolina. She could not take her son with her, so Art, as the family called him, stayed with his grandparents.

He had a good life in Demopolis and his business sense surfaced at a young age. There was a swing in the family's front yard, hung from oak trees. It was the only swing in town. Art noticed how all the neighborhood children liked to come over to swing, and he decided to charge them for the chance. He was not discouraged by the fact that the children had no money. He had them pay with buttons, and collected them in a cigar box. He converted his "earnings" into cash by taking the box of buttons to a woman who sewed for a living. She would buy the buttons from him.

It was not long after that first business success that Art went to live in Birmingham, Alabama. His mother's employer owned a store there and wanted her to continue working for his family. She would have an apartment above the barn behind their house and arranged for Art to come live with her. He had mixed emotions on leaving his grandparents, for they meant a lot to him. So did the warmth and security of their home. Yet he felt a sense of adventure. He had heard of Birmingham and wondered what it would be like living there.

His mother's employer had a son about Art's age. The two boys spent many hours playing together. There were no black schools nearby, yet Art's mother wanted her son to get an education. She knew of a boarding school called Tuggle Institute in Birmingham. Its founder was Mrs. Carrie Tuggle, whom the children called "Granny Tuggle." It was from her that Art Gaston learned how it was possible to accomplish a lot with a little money.

Booker T. Washington, the president of Tuskegee Institute, was another person who made an impact on A. G. Gaston. In a speech he made at Tuggle Institute, Washington stressed the importance of grasping opportunities at the right moment.

When Art completed his education at Tuggle, he felt it was time for him to make some decisions. He had limited choices. He knew he didn't have enough money to continue his education at Tuskegee. World War I was brewing. He surveyed the local job situation. There was no job available that would pay as much as the $15 a month he could get in the Army. So he enlisted. Before he left Birmingham, he went to a bank and arranged to buy a lot where he hoped to build a home after the war. He would have his paycheck sent to the bank as payments on the property.

Gaston was fortunate to survive harrowing experiences serving with the Army forces in France. Death and destruction were all around. On returning to the United States, he finished his service time at Camp Bowie, Texas. After his discharge he stopped to visit friends in Meridian, Mississippi, on his way to rejoin his family in Alabama. These were the Smiths whom he had known from childhood days in Demopolis. Mr. Smith now had a thriving blacksmith business. Art had known their daughter, Creola, for as long as he could remember.

In Birmingham he found out that his mother now was in

business for herself, working as a caterer. She had rented a small house on 8th Avenue North. Art Gaston expected to be able to go out the next morning and find a job, but discovered that was impossible. Eventually, he found steady work at the Tennessee Coal and Iron Company in Westfield, Alabama. He earned $3.10 a day, and inexpensive housing was available to the workers. He moved his mother and elderly grandmother to a small house close to his work.

Being a laborer in a coal mine was exhausting work and Art Gaston still dreamed of becoming a businessman. One day at lunchtime he had a brainstorm that turned into a successful business. Like all of his ideas, it grew out of his ability to study the people around him. He noticed that the other workers were always eager to see what he had in his lunchbox. Many of the men had no families and ate store-bought items. They would much rather have the fried chicken, sweet potatoes, and biscuits that Art's mother provided him. He decided to ask his mother to prepare box lunches for sale. She did, and soon they had a booming business.

With his income from the Tennessee Coal and Iron Company and the lunch business, Art Gaston was finally able to save some money. He put himself on a strict budget. Some of the other workers were less frugal and tried to borrow money between paydays. A. G. Gaston was willing to lend it—with interest, of course.

He noticed something else happening on paydays. Solicitors would come to ask for money to pay burial expenses for family members who died. The workmen were generous in donating, and that set A. G. Gaston to thinking again. Why not start his own burial society?

A. G. Gaston in front of bank he founded in Birmingham

He discussed his idea with Granny Tuggle and with ministers and coworkers he respected. All thought it was a good idea. He succeeded in getting lots of people to join, charging twenty-five cents for the head of a household and ten cents for any additional family members. He knew that burials cost about $100 and felt pretty sure no one would die before he had collected at least that much.

But then a woman died the week after she joined. She had paid in just thirty-five cents. He was faced with a dilemma. She had signed up with his burial society in good faith. He asked one of the ministers he had consulted if he would have his church take up a collection to pay for the burial, but was refused.

He talked with James Payne, who operated a local funeral home. Payne agreed to reduce the rate to $75. Then, to Gaston's surprise, the minister conducting the funeral told the congregation they could contribute "coins of comfort." He also described the benefits of Gaston's burial society and how the woman had paid only thirty-five cents. There was enough money collected to pay the undertaker.

The burial business grew and branched out to other towns. Gaston named it the Booker T. Washington Burial Society in honor of a friend who had the same name as the president of Tuskegee Institute.

Art Gaston soon had financial security and felt he was ready to ask Creola Smith to marry him. He went to Meridian to ask her, and she accepted. Her father objected at first, but relented if Creola would agree to finish college.

The newlyweds first lived in Westfield, and Creola enthusiastically supported her husband in his business. A near-disaster in a coal mine made Gaston determined not to go back to the mines, and since the Booker T. Washington Burial Society was doing well, he began to devote full time to it. The couple moved to Fairfield, and the Society was formally organized, with Gaston as president, Creola's father as vice-president, and Creola as secretary. When the undertaker they had been working with ran into problems, they bought his funeral home and promptly named it Smith and Gaston.

Not long after, the burial society became the Booker T. Washington Insurance Company. The next step was to let more people know about it. They sponsored the first regular black radio programs, and promoted live musical extravaganzas in Birmingham. Thousands of people attended.

A. G. Gaston learned the value of saving money through his experience in taking out a loan that would enable his insurance company to qualify with the state insurance department. He had to repay the loan with 10 percent of the business' income and when it was paid off, he continued to save the 10 percent. He concluded that saving was the secret to success. His slogan became "A part of all you earn is yours to keep."

Although business was good, Gaston had other worries. Both Creola and her father were seriously ill. In addition, the mayor of Fairfield resented the fact that Mr. Smith had encouraged black townspeople to register and vote. He started a harrassment campaign. Rather than face that situation, Gaston decided to leave Fairfield and get established in Birmingham.

He and John Commons, a black man who had made money selling coal and ice, shared the cost of buying a mansion. Gas-

A. G. Gaston pictured with his portrait and a
photograph of his childhood home.

ton would use part of the space for his business and Commons would receive income from rental apartments. During the renovation period, Creola's health and also her father's worsened. Neither of them lived to see the grand opening.

Creola's mother hoped Gaston would choose another member of the family for his second wife, but he married Minnie Lee Gardner, a good friend from Fairfield days. She had gone to Tuskegee and her training complemented his work.

As the insurance company and funeral home businesses grew, more office workers were needed. A. G. Gaston hired a young man from Chicago to give on-the-job training to his employees. But recognizing a real need for office skills, he established a business college. He knew the perfect person to be the director: Minnie Lee Gardner Gaston.

The Gastons liked to travel, and with the businesses well organized and well staffed, they could get away. A. G. Gaston was the official delegate of the African Methodist Episcopal Church to the World Ecumenical Conference in Oxford, England. While there, he learned that the National Baptist Convention would probably meet in Birmingham the following year. The thousands of delegates would mean business for the city, but Gaston knew that housing would be a problem. The "separate but equal" laws would prevent black people from staying in white-owned hotels. He solved the problem by following his "find a need and fill it" rule. He decided to build a motel that would be open to guests of any race. The 65-unit motel had a pool, restaurant, and lounge. Dr. Martin Luther King, Jr., who attended the convention, had his Birmingham headquarters at the Gaston Motel.

In later years, Gaston saw the need for a real estate company, two cemeteries, two radio stations, a construction company, a housing development, a drug store. He served on many boards of directors. His advice was sought by the White House. He dined with Presidents John F. Kennedy and Lyndon B. Johnson.

Gaston initiated many programs for young people. In addition to the A. G. Gaston Boys' and Girls' Club, he organized the statewide A. G. Gaston Spelling Bee, with college scholarships for promising young men and women.

A. G. Gaston died January 19, 1996, at the age of 103. He saw many changes throughout his long, productive life, but demonstrated that it is possible to accomplish seemingly impossible things. John Johnson, publisher of *Jet* and *Ebony*, said of A. G. Gaston, "He blazed a trail in a wilderness of prejudice and racism." Yet A. G. Gaston did not think of himself as an exceptional person. He truly believed what he said: "What I have done anybody can do."

Two Wishes and One Good Idea

CAST

Art Gaston	First Child
"Son," his cousin	Second Child
First Narrator	Third Child
Second Narrator	

FIRST NARRATOR: The setting is the front yard outside a log cabin in Demopolis, Alabama, almost 100 years ago.

SECOND NARRATOR: There's a boy named Arthur George Gaston who lives in that cabin with his grandparents. Arthur George's family and friends call him Art.

FIRST NARRATOR: Art has two wishes. One wish is that he had more friends. The other wish is that he can eventually earn lots of money.

SECOND NARRATOR: One day when Art was feeling lonesome, he thought of a way to make both of his wishes come true. Art's father had put up a swing in the front yard for Art and his friends to enjoy. The swing was a wooden door suspended from two tall oak trees by two strong ropes. It was the only swing in the neighborhood.

FIRST NARRATOR: Art knew that all the children in the neighborhood would be eager to get a ride on the swing. He decided to
get his cousin, whose nickname was "Son," to tell everybody to
come swing for a small fee.

SECOND NARRATOR: The neighborhood children didn't have real
money to spend, but Art figured out a way to make his business
profitable. He would have the children pay him with buttons.
Then he would sell the buttons to a woman in the business of
making clothes. She would pay Art with real money.

SON *(going from the First Child to the Second Child to the Third Child at
one side of the stage)*:   Come on over to Art's yard and swing. It
just costs a button to ride.

FIRST CHILD: Oh, good. We've got lots of buttons at home.

SECOND CHILD: So do we. I love to swing!

THIRD CHILD: Me, too.

FIRST NARRATOR: The children went home to get their buttons and
returned to swing. They follow Son over to the other side of the
stage where Art is standing.

SON *(to Art)*:   Art, you sure had a good idea!

ART: Yeah, it looks like this swing business is going to be a good
one. Son, you have done such a good job of letting folks know
about it. You can swing free.

SON *(to Art)*:   Thanks, Cuz.

FIRST CHILD *(to Art and Son)*:   Hey, you guys stop talking. We want
to swing.

SON: OK. *(He points to where he wants the children to stand.)* Line up right over here and have your "fares" ready when I come to collect 'em.

FIRST NARRATOR: The First, Second, and Third Child line up as if to take turns on a swing.

SECOND NARRATOR: Son walks along and collects the buttons. Once the children have paid, Son yells . . .

SON: All aboard!

SECOND NARRATOR: The children pretend to sit down side by side on the wide swing.

FIRST NARRATOR: Son begins to push them in the swing.

SECOND NARRATOR: The children rock back and forth as if they are swinging.

FIRST CHILD: This is so much fun!

SECOND CHILD: Yeah, there never used to be anything to do around here.

THIRD CHILD: I'm going to save my buttons and come swing every day.

SECOND NARRATOR: Arthur George Gaston smiled contentedly as he watched his first business venture succeed. Neither he nor his customers could have imagined what a successful businessman he would eventually become.

CHARLEMAE ROLLINS

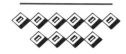

SOMETHING MAGICAL HAPPENED whenever Charlemae Rollins touched the lives of children. And she touched the lives of children in many different ways.

As a storyteller, Charlemae Rollins enchanted her listeners with spellbinding tales of heroes and heroines. As a librarian, she acquainted young readers with books that informed and inspired them. As a lover of language, she encouraged Pulitzer prize-winning poet Gwendolyn Brooks and other young writers to express their thoughts on paper. As a former teacher, she made publishers aware of the need for books that accurately portrayed African Americans. As an expert in this specialized area of literature, she developed guidelines that help librarians, teachers, and parents select books that do not have negative stereotypes. And as an author, she herself wrote six books.

Charlemae Rollins had always been fascinated by stories and books. She credited her grandmother for fostering this fascination. "Grandma told me wonderful stories . . . I've always loved books because of her." This childhood love of books led to her long, successful career as a children's librarian in Chicago. She described her decision to become a librarian as "the best thing I ever did."

Charlemae Hill was born on June 20, 1897, in Yazoo City, Mississippi, the oldest child of Allen G. Hill and Birdie Tucker Hill. Her father was a farmer, her mother a teacher. The Hills moved to the town of Beggs in Oklahoma Territory while Charlemae was quite young. They hoped to find better living conditions there, but were disappointed to find that black children were not allowed to attend the school. Their solution was to establish a school. Charlemae's mother was "one of the first black teachers in . . . Indian Territory."

On completing her elementary education at the new school, Charlemae had to continue her schooling elsewhere because black students could not attend the high schools in Oklahoma. She attended black high schools in St. Louis, Missouri; Holly Springs, Mississippi; and Quindoro, Kansas. Back in Beggs, she passed the teaching exam and taught for a while in her parents' school. Then she left home again for a year at Howard University in Washington, D.C., but returned to Oklahoma to marry Joseph Walter Rollins in April of 1918.

World War I was raging in Europe and soon after the marriage, Joseph Rollins was sent to France with the U.S. Army. Charlemae remained in Oklahoma until he returned from service. Then they made a permanent move to Chicago. In 1920, Joseph Walter Rollins, Jr., was born.

Charlemae's great interest in reading had remained constant through her years as student, teacher, wife, and mother. She applied to the Chicago Public Library and began her career as a children's librarian in 1927. She was first assigned to the Har-

Children's librarian Charlemae Rollins

din Square Branch Library where she worked with children of twenty-six nationalities and soon became known as a wonderful storyteller.

Chicago had a large black community, since many Southern black families moved North to seek better jobs and education. The community had no library until the George Cleveland Hall Branch Library opened in 1932. Charlemae Rollins was selected to be head of the children's department there. This provided her with an opportunity to work with African Americans. She and the library director, Vivian Harsh, made the Hall Branch a cultural center which had an extensive collection of materials by and about black people.

The library was far more than just a place to read. It featured book reviews, discussion groups, lectures, and hobby groups. Published writers like Langston Hughes, Arna Bontemps, Margaret Walker, and Zora Neale Hurston made extensive use of the reference materials at Hall Branch and did much of their writing there. Often they sought out Charlemae Rollins for her advice and encouragement.

Charlemae was particularly good with children—friendly, patient, sympathetic. She provided them with the opportunity to meet real live authors and poets, organized reading, writing, drama, and black history clubs. She visited schools in the neighborhood, and involved parents in reading clinics and encouraged them to take part in parent-teacher groups. And she delighted children and adults, including other librarians, with her storytelling.

Annie Lee Carroll, Yolanda Federici, and Marie Will were three young librarians on whom this great storyteller made a lasting impression. As Annie Lee Carroll explained: "Charlemae Rollins set the pace for us all. She had the ability to get the complete and total respect and attention of her audience.''

Charlemae Rollins was very aware of the power of storytelling. In one of her many articles, entitled ''The Art of Storytelling,'' she stated: ''Storytelling is a wonderful way of breaking down barriers, or getting acquainted with new people, and drawing groups and individuals together.'' Some of Charlemae's stories were ones her grandmother had told her. Some were folk tales she read in books. Still others were based on true stories she found in newspaper articles about achievements of African Americans.

Although Charlemae had compiled a large file of newspaper clippings, she was concerned because very little of this information was available in children's books. She was also concerned that only a few storybooks showed black children as the main characters. Even more disturbing, she found that a large percentage of the relatively few books about African Americans showed inaccurate, negative images. She knew how damaging this could be. And she knew that the situation wouldn't improve unless somebody took action. She determined to be that somebody.

Charlemae was a quiet, gentle woman with a sunny disposition, but almost singlehandedly she challenged two very large, well-established institutions: her employer, the Chicago Public Library, and the entire publishing industry. She encouraged fellow librarians to select books that reflected black life accurately. Although she could make suggestions when she was working directly with other librarians, she didn't have a printed list to give them. With the encouragement of Agatha L. Shea, the Supervisor of Children's Services for the Chicago

Public Library, she compiled a list of books she would rec-
ommend. This became the basis for Charlemae Rollins' first
publication. A booklet entitled *We Build Together* was published
by the National Council of Teachers of English in 1941. This
became an essential resource for librarians all across the United
States.

Meanwhile, Charlemae Rollins wrote letters to publishers
telling them why it was so important to publish books that
reflect the multiracial makeup of American society. She knew
that children of any race would like to learn about the black
inventor Garrett A. Morgan, who invented the stoplight and
made traffic safer for everyone.

Publishers began to respond and started publishing more
books about people of all races and nationalities and to describe them in accurate and respectful terms. Editors and
writers began to ask for Charlemae's advice about book man-
uscripts. Her influence spread and she was widely recognized
for her skill in evaluating books of all kinds. She served on the
Chicago Public Library's advisory committee, and was often
asked to speak at conferences and to conduct workshops in
various sections of the United States. She taught a children's
literature course at Roosevelt University which eventually became a required course for students who were preparing to
teach. She held key leadership positions with the American
Library Association. She served as president of the Children's
Services Division (now ALSC) from 1957 to 1958, the first black
librarian to lead the division. She was chairman of the prestigious Newbery-Caldecott Award Committee in 1956–57. Her
work was recognized in 1972 with an honorary membership
in ALA.

Two master storytellers: Augusta Baker (left) and Charlemae Rollins

As she worked with school groups in and around Chicago, she wished for more books about the African-American experience. She was keenly aware that there were still many untold stories, so she decided to write some children's books herself. She presented the stories of many notable African Americans in *They Showed the Way, Famous Negro Poets,* and *Famous Negro Entertainers of Stage, Screen, and TV.* Her best-known biography is *Black Troubador: Langston Hughes.* For this biography of her longtime friend, Charlemae Rollins won the 1971 Coretta Scott King Award, given for the year's best children's book by an African-American author.

Christmas Gif' is a classic that Charlemae Rollins wrote for readers of every age and nationality. It is a rich collection of black Christmas traditions told through stories, poems, and reminiscences. She delighted audiences whenever she read from it. She also wrote numerous articles for professional library and educational journals. For thirty-six years she served on the advisory committee for the *Bulletin of the Center for Children's Books* published at the University of Chicago.

When Charlemae Rollins chaired the Jane Addams Book Award Committee for the Women's International League for Peace and Freedom, she went to Oslo, Norway, to present the award, which is given for the children's book which best promotes international peace. Her reputation as a master storyteller preceded her. She was a guest of librarians and told stories to children in Norway, Sweden, England, France, and Italy.

She received many acknowledgments of her work during her lifetime. A collection of 2,000 children's books which were displayed at the Seattle World's Fair was donated to Roosevelt University in her name. She received the Grolier Society Award, the Children's Reading Roundtable Award, and the National Book Association's Constance Lindsay Skinner Award. Columbia College of Chicago awarded her an honorary doctorate degree.

On August 29, 1963, Charlemae Rollins retired from her position as children's librarian at the Hall Branch Library.

Charlemae Rollins selects a book.

Throughout her thirty-one years there, she knew and encouraged any number of young people who went on to successful careers. There was John H. Johnson, publisher of *Ebony* and *Jet* magazines, Fred Sanford who became a comedian with the stage name of Redd Foxx, Nat "King" Cole whose songs and piano playing are still popular today, Harold Washington who became the first African-American mayor of Chicago. She also set an example for young people to want to become librarians. Dorothy Evans was one, and she became children's librarian at Hall Branch when Charlemae retired.

Charlemae Hill Rollins died on February 3, 1979. During her final illness, she presented her personal collection of books to the Carter G. Woodson Regional Library. A portrait of her hangs in the Vivian Harsh Room there. Details of her life and work can be found in biographies written by Holly G. Willett and Spencer H. Shaw.

A number of tributes have honored the memory of Charlemae Rollins. In October, 1989, the children's room at the Hall Branch Library was named for her. The Charlemae Hill Rollins Colloquium, sponsored by the School of Library and Information Sciences at North Carolina Central University, was established in 1980 by Dr. Benjamin F. Speller, dean, and Joseph Rollins, Jr., to improve library services to all children. The annual President's Program of the Association for Library Service to Children (a division of the American Library Association) has been named in honor of Charlemae Rollins.

Most of all, her memory is kept alive whenever you hear a great storyteller or read a book that accurately portrays African Americans.

onversation with Langston Hughes

CAST

Mrs. Charlemae Rollins	John
Langston Hughes	Dorothy
Narrator	Nathaniel
Dempsey	Harold
Fred	

Note: You will need a book of Langston Hughes poems. Select the ones to be read.

NARRATOR: The year is 1936. It is a busy Saturday morning at the Hall Branch Library on the southside of Chicago. An audience —which includes students from nearby Jean Baptiste Pointe Du Sable High School—is waiting expectantly for an important meeting to begin. Mrs. Rollins, head of children's services at the library, goes to the front of the room.

MRS. ROLLINS: Good morning! We are in for a real treat today. We're privileged to have Langston Hughes talk with us. He is a very talented writer whom you may have seen working here at the Hall Branch. Today he has taken time out to visit our Negro History Club.

Langston Hughes is often called "the people's poet" because his poems are so down-to-earth. He has also written plays and children's books. What you may not know is that he has lived some real-life adventures that are more exciting than those of some storybook characters. You will get to ask him about these things but, first, he will talk about and read from his poetry.

I'm not going to take any more time. It is my pleasure to introduce Langston Hughes. Won't you give him a big hand?

NARRATOR: As Mrs. Rollins and the audience clap, a young man who has been seated in the audience stands and walks toward the front of the room. He is holding some books and papers in his hands.

LANGSTON HUGHES: Good morning. It is a pleasure to talk with you today. I have seen many of you coming in and out of the library as I've been working on my writing. I'm glad to have this opportunity for us to get better acquainted.

Before I begin reading poems to you, I want to explain something. People often ask me about the rhythm in my poetry. I tell them that poetry is the pulse of life. It is like a heartbeat. I try to capture that sense of rhythm in my poems. Listen for it as I read. *(He reads two or three selections.)*

NARRATOR: Then Langston Hughes says . . .

LANGSTON HUGHES: Now, what questions can I answer for you?

NARRATOR: Dempsey raises his hand. Langston Hughes calls on him.

LANGSTON HUGHES: What is your question, young man?

DEMPSEY: I'm a musician. Do you like jazz and blues?

LANGSTON HUGHES: Yes, I love them.

DEMPSEY: Do they influence your poetry?

LANGSTON HUGHES: Yes, definitely. Music and poetry both have rhythm and movement.

DEMPSEY: How did you get started writing poetry in the first place?

LANGSTON HUGHES: I started writing quite by chance. I had lived in at least six cities by the time I was fourteen. I finished grade school in Lincoln, Illinois. I had never written a poem in my life, but my classmates chose me to be "class poet" because they had heard someone say that black people have rhythm and they knew a poet had to have rhythm. So I was selected and was expected to produce a poem. I did, and everyone liked it.

That got me started writing. We moved again soon after graduation—to Cleveland, Ohio. I wrote for the high school magazine and was editor of the yearbook.

NARRATOR: John raises his hand and when Langston Hughes calls on him, he asks . . .

JOHN: Was anybody else in your family interested in writing?

NARRATOR: Langston Hughes hesitates for a moment, as if John's question has made him recall an old memory.

LANGSTON HUGHES: Yes, my mother used to write poems and do dramatic readings at the Inter-State Library Society founded by her father.

NARRATOR: Langston Hughes pauses again, then continues . . .

LANGSTON HUGHES: As history club members, you will be interested in a couple of other things about my mother's father, who was my grandfather, of course. His name was Charles Langston.

He took part in the daring rescue of a slave who had escaped to Oberlin, Ohio. And he was the brother of the noted lawyer, John Mercer Langston.

NARRATOR: Fred impatiently blurts out a question.

FRED: Were you named Langston after your grandfather and his brother?

LANGSTON HUGHES: Yes, it was their last name and my middle name. I thought it was more unusual than my first name, which is James, so I called myself Langston Hughes.

NARRATOR: Dorothy raises her hand. Langston Hughes calls on her.

DOROTHY: I'd like to go back to something you mentioned earlier. You said you lived in a lot of different places while you were growing up. Is there any one of those places that you really think of as home?

LANGSTON HUGHES: Definitely. I lived with my grandmother—my mother's mother—in Lawrence, Kansas, for a long time. My grandmother used to read to me. That's how I discovered the world of books. I used to entertain myself by reading about interesting storybook characters and wonderful faraway places.

NATHANIEL: When Mrs. Rollins introduced you, she said you had had more exciting real-life adventures than many storybook characters. Would you tell us about one of your adventures?

LANGSTON HUGHES: Yes . . . my father had wanted to become a lawyer. He was so angered by the racial prejudice he encountered when he wanted to take the Oklahoma state bar exam that he left the United States. He eventually settled in Mexico where he could practice law without restrictions. He sent for my mother and grandmother and me. Soon after we arrived in Mexico City there was a tremendous earthquake. The big National Opera House crumbled to the ground. My mother decided that was too much excitement for her. So we packed up and headed back to my grandmother's house in Kansas.

NARRATOR: Harold raises his hand.

HAROLD: My father is a lawyer, and I want to be one too. Did you ever wish to be a lawyer?

LANGSTON HUGHES: No. I knew from a young age that what I wanted to do is write. But I did all kinds of work before I was able to devote my full time to writing.

HAROLD: What kinds of things did you do?

LANGSTON HUGHES: Everything! I was a truck farmer, a cook, a waiter, and even a doorman at a nightclub in Paris, France. I was once an English teacher, and I worked as research assistant to Dr. Carter G. Woodson in Washington, D.C. I was a mess steward on a ship and sailed to West Africa, the Canary islands, and the Azores.

NARRATOR: Mrs. Rollins goes and stands by Langston Hughes.

MRS. ROLLINS: You students have so many questions I can see that we're going to have to invite Langston Hughes back to continue his conversation with the Negro History Club. But before we dismiss for today, I'd like to ask a question I think everybody would like to hear the answer to.

NARRATOR: Turning to Langston Hughes, she asks . . .

MRS. ROLLINS: What long-range project do you have in mind?

LANGSTON HUGHES: One thing I'd really like to do is write a book about outstanding American Negroes. My grandmother used to tell me about contributions black men and women have made to America and the world. I believe everybody deserves to know about them, so I guess I'll have to write the book.

MRS. ROLLINS: Thank you, Langston. We need a book like that. I also think there ought to be a book about you, because you certainly are an outstanding young man. And, if I may make a prediction, I wouldn't be surprised if some of the young people in this audience do some pretty outstanding things when they grow up.

NARRATOR: Those were prophetic words. Some years later, Langston Hughes did write a book entitled *Famous American Negroes*. And Mrs. Rollins wrote a book entitled *Black Troubadour: Langston Hughes*. And her prediction about the students came true.

- Dempsey Travis started out as a musician, then became successful in real estate and wrote several books.

- John H. Johnson became the publisher of *Ebony* and *Jet* magazines and wrote his autobiography.

- Fred Sanford became a comedian who starred in two television series. His stage name was Redd Foxx.

- Dorothy Donegan became an internationally acclaimed jazz pianist.

- Nat "King" Cole became a singer and pianist whose popularity continues long after his death.

- Harold Washington became a lawyer, a state legislator, a U.S. Congressman, and eventually the first African-American mayor of Chicago.

Bessie Coleman

BESSIE COLEMAN didn't believe the old saying, "The sky's the limit." Instead, she believed the sky offered limitless possibilities to anyone with enough daring and determination to soar. She overcame many obstacles and earned an international pilot's license years before the well-publicized flights of Charles Lindbergh and Amelia Earhart.

The new field of aviation had captured the imagination of the entire world. For centuries, people had had a fascination with the flight of birds and had tried to devise different ways to become airborne. Inventors had constructed lightweight gliders and hot air balloons, but it was the invention of powered "flying machines" that began a new era.

The early "flying machines" were fragile, compared to today's airplanes. They were made of wood, braced by wires, and covered with cloth that had been painted with varnish. Most were biplanes (with an upper and lower wing). Many were "two-seaters" with dual controls. They flew at what would be considered low altitudes today. Speeds ranged from 65 to 130 miles per hour

Few men and fewer women of any race were pilots. A true

pioneering spirit was essential for anyone venturing into the exciting new world of aviation. Pilots had no elaborate flight charts. They used road maps and followed railroad tracks instead. They used lakes, towns, cities, highways, farms, and water towers as navigation aids. Often, if a pilot ran low on fuel, he or she landed on a rural highway or in a field. Mechanical problems frequently caused emergency landings—some of which were successful and some of which were not.

Most often, pilot training was done by one pilot giving private lessons to a person who wanted to learn how to fly. Eventually, this practice was expanded and small flying schools were formed.

At the beginning of this pioneering period of aviation, pilots were not required to have licenses. In 1905, nine European countries organized the Federation Aeronautique Internationale to establish guidelines for world aviation and to keep records on how far or how fast planes flew. Even after the Federation was established, an FAI license was not legally required, but it was sought by pilots as undisputable proof of their flying ability. Although the FAI was based in France, it permitted flying clubs in the United States to issue FAI licenses to their members.

Bessie Coleman realized that aviation would not be an easy field to enter. She was aware that women applicants often met with resistance when they tried to enroll in flight training. Being an African American who grew up while racial segregation was legal in the South and practiced elsewhere in America, she already knew what it was like to be kept from participating in some things that interested her. She had not heard of any African American—man or woman—who had taken flight training in the United States. Even so, she was eager to enter the exciting field of aviation.

Bessie applied to one flight school after another. All of her applications were turned down. When she told Robert S. Abbott, founder of the *Chicago Defender* newspaper, of her disappointment, he made contact with a French flying school that would train her. He then suggested that she learn French. She did, and mastered the language.

As a result, Bessie Coleman became the first American woman to earn an international pilot's license in the country where the prestigious Federation Aeronautique Internationale had its headquarters. People who knew Bessie Coleman said that she was born with the desire to "do something with her life." But they couldn't have predicted that she would do something so remarkable.

Bessie was a child laboring in a Texas cotton field on that December day in 1903 when Orville and Wilbur Wright made their historic flight at Kitty Hawk, North Carolina. There has been some question about just how old she was at the time. Most writers have used January 26, 1893, as her birth date, but she listed January 20, 1896, on both her international pilot's license and her passport. It would seem that she would give the correct date on those important documents.

What Bessie Coleman's biographers do agree on is that she was born in Atlanta, Texas. She was a toddler when her parents, George and Susan Coleman, moved to Waxahachie, a small town about thirty miles from Dallas. She was one of thirteen children, nine of whom lived to adulthood.

Although her parents owned the land they lived on, times were hard. In the late 1890s, depressed economic conditions and racial barriers presented tremendous obstacles for African-American families in the rural South. Reports reached many of these families that living conditions were better in what is present-day Oklahoma, a portion of which was then known as "Indian Territory." Many black people in former Confederate states decided to move to the Territory. This was especially true of African Americans who—like Bessie's father, George Coleman—also had Native-American ancestry.

Bessie's mother, Susan Coleman, did not join her husband when he moved to the Territory. She preferred the familiar Texas surroundings. She and the children picked cotton, and she took in laundry. As the children got older, they helped with the washing and ironing. Bessie was assigned the task of keeping a written record of the money earned.

Schools for black children in the rural South were seasonal. They closed during harvest season when children were expected to work in the fields. Although Susan Coleman did not know how to read, she encouraged her children to enjoy books. Once or twice a year a wagon library came to town. The Coleman children looked forward to borrowing books they could keep until the wagon returned.

Bessie especially enjoyed reading. Each evening she read aloud to the rest of her family, sometimes from the Bible or from biographies of black heroes and heroines. She read the poetry of Paul Laurence Dunbar, and discovered that he published a newspaper that was printed by the Wright brothers before they began to fly. She read about Booker T. Washington and Harriet Tubman, and realized that it was possible to make changes in one's life.

Bessie was determined to do something significant with her own life. She knew she would need more schooling. She managed to complete high school, but hoped to go on to college. Her mother encouraged her, but could not afford to pay the tuition. Instead, she allowed Bessie to stop contributing to family finances and to save the money she earned from washing and ironing clothes.

Bessie's savings enabled her to go to Langston Industrial College in Oklahoma. Her money ran out after one semester, however. Even so, she had been able to accomplish so much more than most students that members of her church gave her a warm homecoming. While it was nice to be home with family and friends, Bessie knew she did not want to spend her life picking cotton or taking in laundry. She decided to join her brother, John, in Chicago and get a job and work her way through school.

She was soon attending Burnham's School of Beauty Culture. After receiving her certificate, she found work as a manicurist at a barbershop. She entered a competition for manicurists, and sent her family an article from the *Chicago Defender* showing her giving the winning manicure. She took a second job—managing a chili parlor—and saved enough money to make it possible for her mother and other family members to move from Texas to Chicago.

The year was 1919. World War I had been over less than a year. Airplanes had played an unexpectedly significant role in the war, and people were amazed by the flying machines and their daring pilots. Bessie Coleman shared this interest. She decorated the barbershop window with a model airplane a child had given her. She read everything she could find about planes and pilots. She found out about a few American women who were pilots—Harriet Quimby and Katherine and Marjorie Stinson. She read of two black inventors, James F. Adams who held a U.S. patent for "Propelling Means for Aeroplanes" and John F. Pickering who had patented an airship in 1900. The more Bessie read, the more certain she became that she wanted to enter the field of aviation.

Bessie's brother John was a veteran of World War I. He and his friends took pride in talking about the valor of black troops in the war. They spoke with pride of Eugene Bullard, a black pilot who earned the French Legion of Honor medal. Bessie and John's niece, Marion Coleman, said, "Uncle Johnny was a big tease and he told Aunt Bessie, 'Woman in France are flying planes while you're sitting up here polishing fingernails!' " Bessie was more determined than ever to learn to fly. But no American training programs would admit her. And then Robert Abbott made it possible for her to be accepted in France.

She was delighted when she received a letter informing her she had been admitted to flight school in LeCrotoy, France, near Paris. Upon receiving this good news, she went to her bank to withdraw money for travel and training. Knowing how new and dangerous aviation was at that time, Jesse Binga, the banker—and her family—discouraged this. Although Bessie realized that they meant well, she assured them this was right for her, and soon set sail for Europe.

Her studies were all that Bessie Coleman would have wished

Aviation pioneer Bessie Coleman

for. She flew by day and read each night. She learned the history, the dynamics, and the how-to of flying. She logged many hours at the controls of the most advanced aircraft of the times. She received lessons from accomplished European flight instructors. One of her aviation mentors was the famed aircraft designer, Anthony H. G. Fokker.

She received an international pilot's license on June 15, 1921. It was a dream come true. Now that she had her license, she was eager to share her knowledge. She was especially anxious to encourage people of African descent to participate in the limitless possibilities created by the world of aviation. She remained in France long enough to communicate this idea at the Second Pan-African Congress. She returned to the United States in September, 1921, the first American woman to earn an FAI license issued in France. But the racial barriers which prevented her from being admitted to flight school affected the reception she received when she returned home. Instead of being heralded for her spectacular personal achievement and the honor she had brought to her country, she was practically ignored by much of the national press. She was featured in the black press, however, and was warmly welcomed by people who learned of her accomplishment in this way.

Bessie immediately began working on plans to open a flying school. She knew it would take money, and soon learned that investors were hard to find.

Bessie Coleman staged her first exhibition at Curtiss Field in New York on Labor Day weekend of 1922. It drew a large, enthusiastic crowd and prompted a number of young black men to ask where they could take flying lessons. The next month she staged her first Chicago area show at Checkerboard Field near the village of Maywood. The *Chicago Defender* newspaper gave the event extensive publicity. Thousands of people came out to see the world's only black woman pilot put on a solo show. Colonel Otis B. Duncan, Commander of the 8th Regiment of the Illinois National Guard was there. According to Bessie's sister, Elois, "The highlight of the event came when Bessie took Colonel Duncan up for a flight and made the figure eight, banked, and made several low dips before landing."

Giving air shows wasn't the only way Bessie Coleman tried to acquaint people with aviation. She spoke at city and suburban churches and theaters. She was determined to open flight training to black people in America, and was undaunted when she could not find sponsors who would invest enough money for her to open a school. She decided that if she could

Bessie Coleman with her airplane

not find financial backers, she could raise the money herself. She would do it by becoming a "barnstormer," a pilot who went from town to town showing off his ability as a flyer. Barnstormers often took great chances in performing stunts, and crowds were as interested in seeing accidents as in seeing skillful flying. As preparation, Bessie Coleman went back to France for advanced training. She had courses in stunt flying and parachute jumping.

On returning to the United States, her plan was to rent or borrow planes to use in her air shows. Unable to find airplane owners who would agree to this arrangement, she reportedly used her remaining savings to buy three Army surplus planes. She put on exhibitions in cities across the South from Florida to Texas, delighting onlookers with her stunt flying. Once when a parachutist failed to show up, Bessie Coleman turned the controls over to her copilot, then she parachuted from the plane. She expanded her territory, staging air shows from Massachusetts to California. She paid tribute to her role model, Harriet Quimby, by giving an exhibition over the Charles River in Cambridge, Massachusetts, at the site where, in 1912, Harriet Quimby catapulted out of her plane and fell to her death. Harriet received her training at a New York flying school and was the first woman pilot to be licensed in the United States.

Gradually, Bessie Coleman began to get increased recognition. She was featured in movie newsreels, and did some advertising for the Firestone Rubber Company. She had an accident in California which sidelined her for about a year. Her plane malfunctioned and crashed a few minutes after takeoff. She suffered broken ribs, facial cuts, and a fracture of her left leg. This was only a temporary setback, however. She announced to the world, "I'm coming back!"

When she recuperated, she resumed her efforts to establish a flight school. Still unable to get enough big companies or wealthy people to invest in the school, she resumed barnstorming in order to earn money. On May Day, 1926, she was to give an air show for the Negro Welfare League of Jacksonville, Florida. Arriving a day early, she had dinner that evening at the same restaurant as newspaper publisher Robert Abbott. Bessie introduced him to her friends, saying, "This is the man who gave me my chance. I shall never forget him." For some reason, Robert Abbott tried to talk Bessie Coleman into cancelling her exhibition. She assured him she would be all right.

Her copilot, William Wills, had flown their plane in from Texas. He had experienced mechanical problems and had made two forced landings en route. After repairs were made, he and Bessie believed the plane was safe to fly. But when they went up for a test flight, the plane malfunctioned again. Although Bessie Coleman was usually careful to wear a seat belt, that day she either failed to wear one or it broke. She, like Harriet Quimby, was thrown out of the plane to her death. Her copilot was killed as he attempted to land the plane.

News of Bessie Coleman's death reached Chicago quickly. Within an hour, the *Defender* newspaper had a special edition out with the headline: "Girl Flyer Killed In Plane Fall." Black businesses displayed pictures of Bessie Coleman in their windows.

Each spring, on the Saturday closest to the anniversary of Bessie Coleman's death, black pilots pay their respects. They

*Bessie Coleman's international pilot's
license issued on June 15, 1921.*

*U.S. postage stamp honoring
Bessie Coleman*

fly in V-formation over Lincoln Cemetery and drop a wreath of flowers to be placed on her grave. This annual flyover was started in the 1930s by the Challenger Air Pilots Association led by Cornelius Coffey. The tradition was continued by the Chicago American Pilots Association under the direction of aviation historian Rufus A. Hunt. Family and friends participate in a commemorative program near her gravesite prior to the flyover, and a proclamation from the city of Chicago is read. In the mid-1990s it was expanded to honor all black women flyers.

Tributes to Bessie Coleman are also held in Jacksonville, Florida. In 1986, Mrs. Mattie Eiland's students at the Bradwell School in Chicago had a Bessie Coleman Day for the entire school. They prepared skits, wrote songs, and wore Bessie Coleman shirts. The idea has since been adopted by other schools.

Members of the Bessie Coleman Research Team at Miami University in Ohio conducted extensive research and even went to France to retrace Bessie Coleman's steps. They developed materials for schools and helped circulate petitions for a Bessie Coleman stamp.

On April 27, 1995, the United States Post Office issued the Bessie Coleman postage stamp in its Black Heritage series. A reception and program were held at the DuSable Museum of African-American History the previous evening. First Day of Issue ceremonies were held at Midway Airport in Chicago. Hundreds of schoolchildren, aviation enthusiasts, and stamp collectors gathered for the occasion. Postmaster Rufus Porter and Bessie Coleman's niece, Marion, spoke. Eighteen-year-old Nia Gilliam was the lead pilot in the V-formation salute.

Bessie Coleman has been honored in other ways. A Chicago public library is named for her. A group of African-American women flyers, headed by Joyce Givens, was called the Bessie Coleman Flying Club. At O'Hare Airport the first road sign that passengers see as they go from the airport toward downtown Chicago is Bessie Coleman Drive. The Bessie Coleman Foundation is based at the St. Galacius Catholic Church in Chicago.

In Washington, D.C., her role in aviation is acknowledged in the Black Wings and the African Americans in Aviation exhibits at the National Air and Space Museum. Her pilot's license from Federation Aeronautique Internationale is in the DuSable Museum in Chicago. She is honored in the Women in Aviation exhibit at the San Diego Aerospace Museum.

Bessie Coleman's pioneering spirit continues to be an inspiration. She entered aviation in its early days and charted her own course. She not only wanted to be personally involved, she wanted to provide opportunities for other African Americans. Although Bessie Coleman did not do all the things she had hoped to do, she was a trailblazer. Her ability to set a goal and work toward it would have enabled her to excell in any field.

A Day to Remember

CAST

First Narrator   First Spectator
Second narrator   Second Spectator
Phyllis   Third Spectator
Claude   Announcer
Aunt Susie

FIRST NARRATOR: Imagine that you're at Checkerboard Airfield near Maywood, Illinois, on October 15, 1922.

SECOND NARRATOR: You are about to witness a breathtaking air show put on by none other than Bessie Coleman, the first black woman pilot in the world.

FIRST NARRATOR: Publicity in the *Chicago Defender* newspaper has drawn a huge, enthusiastic crowd.

SECOND NARRATOR: There are at least 2,000 people in the bleachers. This is during the early days of aviation and the spectators are eager not only to see an air show, but to see a young Chicago woman at the controls.

FIRST NARRATOR: The band is playing and vendors are selling their wares as the spectators wait for the show to begin.

POPCORN VENDOR: Popcorn. Popcorn.
                 Buttery and hot.
                 Buy a bag.
                 You'll like it a lot.

PHYLLIS (*to her aunt*):   Aunt Susie, I can't see everything from here. Can I go stand in front of the crowd?

AUNT SUSIE (*pointing to an opening in the crowd*):   Yes, but stand right there by the fence so you won't get lost in the crowd.

PHYLLIS: All right.

AUNT SUSIE (*to Phyllis*):   Here's some spending change. You may want to buy some popcorn.

PHYLLIS: Thanks, Aunt Susie.

SECOND NARRATOR: Phyllis makes her way to the front row of spectators.

FIRST NARRATOR: She finds herself standing next to a boy who's about her age.

SECOND NARRATOR: He's been watching Bessie Coleman check over her plane. She is wearing a leather helmet and goggles. Her military style uniform has a wide leather belt and a strap over one shoulder.

CLAUDE (*pointing to Bessie Coleman as he speaks to Phyllis*):   Look, there's Bessie Coleman. I can't believe I'm going to get to see her fly. She used to manicure people's fingernails at a shop around the corner from where I live.

PHYLLIS: Really? I don't know that much about her.

CLAUDE: How could you be from around Chicago and not know much about Bessie Coleman?

PHYLLIS: I'm not from here. I live in Springfield and I just came up here to visit my aunt.

CLAUDE: Oh, I see. Well, I sell the *Defender* newspaper. Every week it runs pictures and stories about Bessie Coleman.

PHYLLIS: You know about Bessie Coleman, but did you know that a military man from Springfield is going up in the plane with her?

CLAUDE: No, I didn't know anybody was going to fly with her. Who is the man?

PHYLLIS: His name is Col. Otis B. Duncan. I know him from . . .

CLAUDE: You know him?

PHYLLIS: Yes, I see him every Sunday at the Culture Club.

CLAUDE: The Culture Club? What's that?

PHYLLIS: It's a neighborhood meeting. Students from the Springfield schools get together at the Baptist church to read our best school papers. Colonel Duncan is one of the grownups who comes to hear us and encourage us.

FIRST NARRATOR: Phyllis and Claude's voices are drowned out by the announcer.

ANNOUNCER: Ladies and gentlemen, boys and girls. You are about to see a spectacular event. Chicago's own Bessie Coleman will demonstrate her remarkable flying skills. She has just recently returned to the United States after receiving her international pilot's license in France. To my knowledge, she is the first American, male or female of any race, to do so. Please greet Miss Bessie Coleman!

SECOND NARRATOR: With that, Bessie Coleman waves at the crowd and gets into her airplane. She adjusts her goggles and the announcer continues . . .

ANNOUNCER: Joining Miss Coleman today is Col. Otis B. Duncan, Commander of the 8th Regiment of the Illinois National Guard.

FIRST NARATOR: A tall, dark, and handsome Army officer strides over to the plane.

SECOND NARRATOR: Bessie Coleman smiles and shakes Colonel Duncan's hand. He gets into the plane and fastens his seat belt.

FIRST NARRATOR: Bessie starts the plane's engine. The propeller begins to whirl and pretty soon the plane is taxiing down the runway. The crowd is spellbound.

CLAUDE: Wow! Look at that plane go.

PHYLLIS: It's speeding up . . . the wheels are lifting off the ground!

ANNOUNCER: Ladies and gentlemen, boys and girls, you have just witnessed Miss Coleman execute a perfect takeoff. She will now gain altitude and make a pass over the field.

FIRST SPECTATOR: They're flying so high!

SECOND SPECTATOR: Where'd they go? I've lost sight of them.

THIRD SPECTATOR: If you listen, you can hear the plane.

CLAUDE (pointing):   Here they come from way over there.

FIRST NARRATOR: The crowd cheers as the plane makes a pass overhead.

SECOND NARRATOR: The plane swoops back up into the sky.

PHYLLIS: That's fantastic, the way Bessie Coleman can make that plane do whatever she wants it to do.

FIRST NARRATOR: To the crowd's delight, the plane makes another pass.

ALL THREE SPECTATORS *(together)*:   Wow!

CLAUDE: Bessie Coleman is making that plane do a loop!

PHYLLIS: Look, she's going into a second loop.

CLAUDE: She made a figure 8 in the sky!

PHYLLIS: I bet it's in honor of the 8th Illinois Regiment.

SECOND NARRATOR: Everyone in the crowd cheers and claps as Bessie makes a perfect landing.

FIRST NARRATOR *(signaling for the crowd to be quiet)*:   Bessie Coleman and Colonel Duncan wave to the crowd and people in the crowd wave back to them.

ANNOUNCER: Ladies and gentlemen, boys and girls. You have just seen Miss Bessie Coleman demonstrate her splendid flying skills. She says there is a great future in aviation and that she plans to open a flying school where she can train anyone who wants to learn to fly. But you don't have to wait until then. Miss Coleman is giving airplane rides today—for just $1.00 per person. If you want to take an airplane ride, step right over here.

CLAUDE *(reaching into his pocket)*:   I hope I've saved enough money from selling papers to go for a ride.

PHYLLIS *(counting the spending change her aunt gave her):*   I think I have enough money for a ride, but I have to go ask my aunt if I can take a ride.

CLAUDE: I've got to go ask, too. My dad is up in the bleachers with some of his friends.

PHYLLIS: Meet you back here in a few minutes if our folks say OK.

CLAUDE: By the way, what's your name? Mine's Claude.

PHYLLIS: My name is Phyllis. Whether our folks say yes or not, this has been a day I'll always remember.

CLAUDE: Me, too.

Alex Haley

SINCE THE BEGINNING OF TIME, storytellers have held a very special place in cultures all over the world. Traditionally, storytellers have learned, remembered, and told members of each new generation about important people and events in the past.

Alex Haley continued this age-old tradition, but he reached his audience in a way that was different from that of the earliest storytellers. Instead of gathering a relatively small group of listeners around a campfire and using his voice to tell his story, Alex Haley told his stories to millions of people through books and television.

Alex Haley's story, *Roots: The Saga of an American Family*, informed, entertained, and inspired readers and viewers around the world. It was published in book form in 1976. The following year it was made into a highly successful television mini-series.

The story was based on the real and imagined experiences of Alex Haley's own family. It began with his great-great-great-great-grandfather, Kunta Kinte, who was born on the West Coast of Africa in 1750. It ended seven generations and 200 years later when Alex Haley was a grown man. In the intervening years Kunta Kinte's descendants had endured and survived slavery in America and made something of their lives as freed men and women.

Although *Roots* focused on one specific African-American family, it had universal appeal. It touched deep human feelings in people of every race. They could readily identify with Kunta Kinte's feeling of distress upon being kidnapped from his boyhood home in Africa, his frustration at being chained down in the hold of a slave ship, his humiliation at being enslaved on his arrival in North America, and his attempt to keep his self-respect and memories of his African homeland.

People who read the book or saw the TV mini-series gained new insights into aspects of American history. If a person had read about slavery in a textbook, he or she still may not have realized how demoralizing it could be to slaves and to slave-holders. Readers and viewers of *Roots* cheered, gasped, laughed, and cried as they followed the experiences of Kunta Kinte, his daughter, Kizzy, and her son, Chicken George. They were grateful to Alex Haley for bringing them his story.

Schoolchildren wrote him letters. Strangers stopped him on the street to thank him for writing the book. Five hundred colleges designed courses based on *Roots*. Americans from all over the world became interested in tracing their own family roots. They searched for family records in dusty attics, in the National Archives, and in courthouses near where their families had lived. They visited old homesites and family burial grounds. They organized family reunions and interviewed older members of their families. Many grandchildren really got to know their grandparents for the first time.

Alex Haley autographing a copy of his book

Older family members sometimes revealed never-before-talked-about chapters of family history. This was especially true in African-American families. Many of them had felt shame if some of their relatives had been slaves. *Roots* made them feel more comfortable discussing even painful topics. And *Roots* was meaningful to black families in other ways. In the opening scenes, viewers saw family life and culture in Africa before millions of its people were transported to America and enslaved. Later scenes showed how Kunta Kinte and his descendants sought freedom and survived hardships, how they maintained family relationships and a hopeful attitude toward life. This was so inspiring that many young parents named their babies after Kunta Kinte and other characters in *Roots*.

In the first 175 days following its publication, 1,500,000 hardcover copies of *Roots* were sold. When the book appeared in paperback, four million copies were sold. It was translated into 37 languages. The phenomenal success of the book altered Alex Haley's life. He became an instant celebrity. And the book brought him literary honors. In 1977, he won both the National Book Award and the Pulitzer Prize.

The TV series ran for a total of twelve hours over eight consecutive nights. It was more successful than anyone could have predicted. It is estimated that 130 million people viewed at least part of the series. *USA Today* called it "the most watched TV mini-series of all time." This convinced the television industry that a well-told story could keep viewers interested night after night, and the mini-series became a standard TV format.

Alex Haley was an established writer before he wrote *Roots.* He had written stories and articles for *The New York Times Magazine, Atlantic Monthly, Harper's,* and *Reader's Digest.* He also wrote the as-told-to *Autobiography of Malcolm X.*

Much of his writing was based on personal interviews, but it wasn't as a professional interviewer that he first learned the story of his family. When he was just four or five years old, he heard it on his grandmother's front porch in Henning, Tennessee. As an adult, it was the memory of those stories he'd heard from his grandmother, Cynthia Murray Palmer, and her sisters that set him on a search to learn everything he could about his family history. It became a search that continued for twelve years. It involved research on three continents—North America, Africa, and Europe.

Alex Haley's full name was Alexander Murray Palmer Haley. He was born in Ithaca, New York, but spent most of his boyhood at his grandparents' home in Henning, Tennessee. He was the oldest son of Simon and Bertha Palmer Haley, who had met while students at Lane College in Jackson, Tennessee. At the time of Alex's birth on August 11, 1921, his parents were living in New York because his father had earned a graduate scholarship to Cornell University School of Agriculture. When Alex was six weeks old, his parents took him to Henning. He and his mother stayed there while his father finished his studies at Cornell.

Bertha Palmer Haley was the first college graduate in her family. She played the piano very well and taught school in Henning. Alex's grandparents, Will and Cynthia Palmer, took loving care of him. Some of his happiest early memories were of days spent with his grandfather at the W. C. Palmer Lumber Company. Alex was four when his grandfather died. He and his grandmother were distraught. They became extremely close as they both grieved for his grandfather.

His Grandma Cynthia tried to shake off her sadness by inviting her sisters and a cousin to visit. Each evening these ladies would gather on the porch and tell family stories—including that of their African ancestor, Kunta Kinte. Alex was intrigued.

Alex's parents had two more sons, George and Julius. His mother died when Alex was ten or eleven. His father finished his studies and operated the family lumber business for a while. Then he took up the work he most wanted to do—teaching. He taught at the Agricultural and Mechanical College in Normal, Alabama, and strongly encouraged Alex to plan on becoming a teacher. There was a need for black teachers. But Alex didn't feel he was cut out to be a teacher. He entered college and described the experience this way: "I stumbled my way through two years at Alcorn College in Mississippi."

Finally, Simon Haley became convinced that Alex needed time to mature, and got him into the U.S. Coast Guard. It was during his years with the Coast Guard that Alex Haley began his career as a writer. After work each day he would write suitable love letters for his shipmates to send to their girlfriends back home. Alex interviewed the sailors, asking what they wanted their letter to say. He would reword their thoughts into well-written letters. They were so pleased with this arrangement that they paid $1.00 per letter.

That is what made Alex Haley think he could earn money

by writing. He began writing adventure stories and articles. His daytime job was as a cook, but he could write at night. Finally, after hundreds of attempts, he began to sell some of his stories to magazines, and at the end of his three-year tour of duty he reenlisted. Eventually, he became such a skillful writer that the U.S. Coast Guard recognized his ability by creating the position of Chief Journalist especially for him.

He was honorably discharged in 1959 after twenty years of service, and became a free-lance journalist. He became an interviewer for *Reader's Digest* and *Playboy* magazines. Many of his interviews were with people in the news—trumpeter Miles Davis, Nazi leader George Lincoln Rockwell, Dr. Martin Luther King, Jr., and Malcolm X. He always tried to learn as much as he could about the person he would be interviewing, and traveled extensively to do so.

He did a lot of his research at museums, libraries, and archives where important documents are kept. While in London on a writing assignment, he visited the British Museum and saw the Rosetta Stone. He knew it was an important decoding device and decided to find out more about it. When it was found in the Nile River delta, researchers did not understand the Egyptian hieroglyphic writings on it. But they knew how to read one of the three languages on the Rosetta Stone. Gradually they were able to figure out the meaning of the other languages and decipher the hieroglyphics.

Learning this gave Alex Haley an idea. In the family stories he'd heard from his grandmother and her sisters, they often spoke of their African ancestor, Kunta Kinte, who taught his daughter, Kizzy, words from the language he had spoken in

Africa. "Ko" and "Kamby Bolongo" were among the words that Kizzy learned and passed down to her descendants. Alex Haley thought if he could find out what those words meant—and what language they were from—he might learn what tribe Kunta Kinte belonged to or where he lived before being kidnapped and enslaved.

It had been thirty years since Alex had heard these stories. He wasn't sure he remembered all the details, so he sought out the last living family member of his grandmother's generation. That was Cousin Georgia Anderson, who lived in Kansas City. She had sat on the porch with his grandmother and her sisters, and although they told her she was too young to know much about "the old days," she had listened. She told Alex all she knew, then encouraged him to continue his search.

Alex then went to the National Archives in Washington, D.C. He was anxious to see if he could find any documents that mentioned any of his ancestors and sought out the Genealogy Room. He started with the United States Census for 1870. Census records had been kept since 1790, but that was the first year that listed any former slaves by name.

He felt a mounting sense of suspense as he looked for the names of his grandmother's parents, Thomas and Irene Murray. He found them. He even saw the name of his grandmother's oldest sister, Elizabeth, listed. She had been just six years old when the 1870 census was taken. "Seeing their names in the National Archives was wonderous to me," he said later. Finding these family names made him hopeful he would find more written evidence of the relatives he had only heard about.

Little by little, Alex Haley was able to find documents that referred to the family story that took place in America. But he didn't have any information about the part of the story that took place in Africa. What was worse, he didn't know how to go about finding out.

He discussed this dilemma with George Sims, a researcher and a lifelong friend. George Sims provided the names of twelve scholars, known as linguists, who specialized in African languages. Alex contacted one from the University of Wisconsin, and when the scholar reported his research findings, Alex Haley was satisfied that he had identified the language Kunta Kinte had first spoken. It was a Mandinka language, "Kamby Bolongo" was a river, and "Ko" was a musical instrument. With the help of these word clues, further interviews, and a map, Alex Haley concluded that Kunta Kinte had come from a village on a river in The Gambia. More inquiry led him to believe that village was Juffre.

He knew that throughout black Africa there were elderly storytellers, known as *griots*, who memorized the entire history of their villages and clans. He went to Juffre and sat spellbound as he listened to the *griot* tell the centuries-old history of the village. The *griot* spoke of Kunta Kinte and gave details that matched the stories Alex had heard during his boyhood in Tennessee. When the Gambians learned that he was a descendant of an African who had been taken to America 200 years before, he was given a warm welcome.

The more Alex Haley learned, the more he realized that his family's experiences were not unique. They were similar in many ways to the experiences of most black families in both North and South America and the Caribbean. He realized this

Alex Haley during the filming of "Roots" as a mini-series

was an important, little-known story. He decided to write a book. His own ancestors would be a symbolic saga of all African-American families who were descended from someone like Kunta Kinte and their struggle for freedom. He knew that, whatever their race, all families which had left their homelands and had to adjust to life in a new place could identify with this story.

For Alex, the thought of writing a book that would have meaning for so many people seemed overwhelming. Yet he was determined to do it. He knew he needed much more information. He was eager to get back to the United States and get started. On his return, he learned that Cousin Georgia had died within the very hour he had walked into the village of Juffre. He felt a tremendous sense of responsibility to her and other family members to continue the storytelling tradition.

From research in London, Alex had learned the name of the ship on which Kunta Kinte had sailed, the date it left The Gambia, and the name of the ship's captain. But he still needed to find out when and on what ship Kunta Kinte had arrived in the United States. Documents at the Library of Congress led him to believe that he arrived in Annapolis, Maryland. (This was consistent with family stories. His elderly relatives had always said that Kunta Kinte landed at a place called "Naplis.")

At the Maryland Hall of Records he found additional proof. Archivist Phebe Jacobsen directed him to a microfilm copy of the *Maryland Gazette*. That newspaper had exactly what he was looking for. It convinced him that Kunta Kinte had arrived at the port of Annapolis, Maryland, on September 29, 1767, on a ship called *Lord Ligonier*.

When Alex Haley was ready to begin the actual writing of *Roots*, he knew there was no way he could possibly know all the experiences Kunta Kinte had, nor could he know exactly all the thoughts and feelings of other relatives he had first heard about on his grandmother's front porch. Although *Roots* is based on as much family history as he could find, he had to imagine all the rest of the story. He readily admitted this. He even coined the word "faction" to describe his book, indicating that *Roots* is part fact and part fiction. When he could not get definite proof that something had actually happened, he wrote about what possibly happened. He tried to make the characters seem real by describing them as they might have been.

The publisher of *Roots* marketed it as a nonfiction book, although Alex Haley had stated in the book that it was "faction." Over the years he received criticism for the fiction/nonfiction issue and other matters. Soon after *Roots* was published, he was sued by another author who claimed that some passages in the book were too similar to the other author's work. The two authors settled out of court. Following Alex Haley's death, the *Village Voice* newspaper ran an article which raised questions about how factual *Roots* was. A *Washington Post* article written in response to the *Village Voice* article had the heading "Fact or Fiction He Gave Us All a Family Tree."

Widely credited with popularizing the study of family history, Alex Haley's own life was greatly altered by *Roots*. He became a celebrity. He entertained. He was invited to numerous events. He purchased considerable property. He was in constant demand as a speaker, and traveled and lectured all over the world. He was on a speaking tour when he died February 10, 1992, in Seattle, Washington, at the age of seventy.

He never went back to his life as a free-lance journalist. Instead, he became involved with new endeavors. He participated in the production of the TV sequel to "Roots" called "Roots II." He did a series called "Palmertown" based on his childhood memories. He put together a book entitled *Queen*, which was based on his father's family. It was a mini-series that aired in 1993. Shortly before his death he hosted a series of interviews with African-American filmmakers. He published a short novel about the Underground Railroad called *A Different Kind of Christmas*, and assisted in production of a series of ceramic figurines depicting boyhood memories such as "Walking with Grandpa." He supported nine college students with income from speaking engagements—eight from Tennessee and one from The Gambia, homeland of Kunta Kinte.

Alex Haley was married three times. He was the father of two daughters and a son. Unfortunately, his possessions had to be sold at auction after his death to pay off the debts of his estate. The Children's Defense Fund purchased his farm and continues some of the things—like communication across generations—that meant so much to him.

His funeral was held in Memphis, Tennessee, forty-five miles from his beloved town of Henning. It brought together many of the people and symbols that had been most important in his life. A Coast Guard honor guard was in attendance. Dignitaries, family, and friends shared their fond memories of him.

African farewell ceremony at Alex Haley's funeral. Kpe Lee is the drummer; Mrs. Alex Haley is holding the flag.

Malcolm X's daughter, Attallah Shabazz, read a good-bye letter to him. She was Alex Haley's godchild.

Following the funeral in Memphis, a caravan of cars drove to Henning. A brief memorial service was held at the church

Alex attended as a child. Mourners walked the short distance to his grandparents' home which is now a museum and state historic site. Alex Haley was buried near the porch where he had first heard his family's stories.

During graveside services an American flag was presented by the Coast Guard to Alex Haley's widow, Myran Haley. That was followed by a ceremony planned by friends to symbolize how *Roots* had shown the historic link between Africa and America. Soil brought from Africa was sprinkled, a drum song honored Alex Haley as an African chieftain, a flute solo played the theme music from "Roots." In the African tradition, jubilant, uplifting music was played to symbolize that life must go on.

Porch Stories

◇ ◇ ◇

nice atmosphere

family stories

CAST

First Narrator
Second Narrator
Grandma Cynthia

Grandma's four sisters
Young Alex Haley
Cousin Georgia

FIRST NARRATOR: It's a warm summer evening in Henning, Tennessee.

SECOND NARRATOR: Imagine that you are young Alex Haley sitting on Grandma Cynthia's front porch.

FIRST NARRATOR: Fragrant-smelling honeysuckle vines grow at the front and side of the porch. The lights of fireflies flicker on and off among the honeysuckle vines.

SECOND NARRATOR: Your grandma and her four sisters and a cousin are sitting in tall cane-bottomed rocking chairs. They are all rocking their chairs in unison.

FIRST NARRATOR: You listen in silence as they tell family stories that span many generations.

SECOND NARRATOR: That is what Alex Haley did.

FIRST NARRATOR: He heard the sisters tell stories about their girl-hood days.

SECOND NARRATOR: Although Cousin Georgia was also sitting there on the porch, the sisters did the talking.

FIRST NARRATOR: They had convinced Cousin Georgia that she was too young to know about "the old days."

SECOND NARRATOR: The sisters spoke with pride about the time when their parents, Tom and Irene Murray, and their grandfather who was called "Chicken George" led a wagon train from Alamance County in North Carolina to Henning in western Tennessee.

FIRST NARRATOR: After slavery ended, they had left North Carolina to start a new life in Tennessee.

SECOND NARRATOR: Alex's grandmother and her sisters especially liked to talk about people who'd lived long before they were born.

FIRST NARRATOR: Alex noticed that whenever they spoke of a person named "Miss Kizzy," they spoke in a special, respectful tone of voice.

SECOND NARRATOR: Miss Kizzy was their great-grandmother and the mother of Chicken George. When they spoke of her, their voices sounded almost reverent.

GRANDMA CYNTHIA: Thank goodness for Miss Kizzy. We wouldn't have known a thing about our family if it hadn't been for her.

FIRST SISTER: That's right!

SECOND SISTER: It's a good thing her daddy, Kunta Kinte, told her about his boyhood in Africa . . .

THIRD SISTER: . . . and how he was kidnapped by slave catchers one day when he was out in the forest chopping wood to make a drum.

FOURTH SISTER: I'm glad Kunta Kinte used to take the time to tell her the African names of things . . .

GRANDMA CYNTHIA: . . . like when he pointed to a river, he'd say "Kamby Bolongo."

FIRST SISTER: Yes, and when he pointed to a musical instrument, he'd say "Ko."

SECOND SISTER: It's a good thing Miss Kizzy paid close attention to all the things her daddy told her. She must have been an unusual child to remember all those things.

THIRD SISTER: Wouldn't it have been nice if Miss Kizzy hadn't been sold away from her parents?

FOURTH SISTER: Just think how many more stories she could have learned if she hadn't been sold to that mean old Tom Lea.

GRANDMA CYNTHIA: He sure didn't treat Miss Kizzy right. Neither her nor their son, George.

FIRST SISTER: That's right.

GRANDMA CYNTHIA: Sad thing is, it wasn't unusual for masters to expect slave girls to have babies for them.

SECOND SISTER: At least Miss Kizzy taught her son all the stories and African words her daddy had told to her.

THIRD SISTER: Yes, from the time he was five or six, Miss Kizzy repeated those stories so he'd be sure and remember them.

FOURTH SISTER: Well, he learned his lesson good because he saw to it all his children learned about Kunta Kinte . . .

GRANDMA CYNTHIA: . . . even after Tom Lea started sending him around to train fighting cocks and he earned the name "Chicken George."

FIRST SISTER: That's right.

SECOND SISTER: Every time there was a new baby in the family, Chicken George would gather everybody around and retell the story of their African ancestor.

THIRD SISTER: Then when those babies grew up, they passed the story on to their children.

FOURTH SISTER: It's good our daddy, Tom, was one of those children.

GRANDMA CYNTHIA: Yes, indeed. Otherwise, my little grandson, Alex, would never have known who his people were.

FIRST NARRATOR: Alex loved to hear these stories about his family. He wished he could have known Kunta Kinte and Miss Kizzy.

SECOND NARRATOR: Little did his grandma or her sisters, or even Alex himself, know that he would grow up and tell the family story to millions of people around the world . . .

FIRST NARRATOR: . . . through a book and TV mini-series called "Roots: The Saga of an American Family."

MALCOLM X

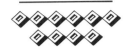

MALCOLM X was a very complex man. "Who *is* Malcolm X?" was frequently asked during his lifetime. "Who *was* Malcolm X?" is still being asked many years after his death. There is no simple answer. Even though Malcolm wrote *The Autobiography of Malcolm X* with author Alex Haley, filmmaker Spike Lee produced a powerful movie about him, and the public bought millions of dollars worth of "X" caps, T-shirts, and books, the questions continue to be asked.

At different periods in his life, Malcolm X was known by different names. As a child his name was Malcolm Little. He was born in Omaha, Nebraska, on May 19, 1925. His parents were Earl and Louise Little, and Malcolm was the fourth of seven children.

Earl Little, originally from Georgia, was a Baptist minister and an organizer for the United Negro Improvement Association (U.N.I.A.), which was headed by Marcus Garvey and encouraged black people to be proud and self-reliant. He was persecuted by whites for his activities. Louise Little was born in Grenada in the British West Indies.

Shortly before Malcolm was born, the family was threatened

by Ku Klux Klan night riders. Earl Little moved his family to Milwaukee, and then to Lansing, Michigan. He resumed his work for the U.N.I.A. and was threatened by a group called the Black Legion that wanted to prevent blacks from going into business for themselves. The Little family experienced what Malcolm later called "the nightmare night." Their house was burned down and the family barely escaped from the showering sparks and flames.

They moved two miles outside of town where Malcolm's father built a four-room house and the family had a garden. One of Malcolm's happiest childhood memories was of having a small garden of his own. In his *Autobiography*, he said, "I would lie down on my back between two rows, and I would gaze up in the blue sky at the clouds moving and think all kinds of things."

Malcolm was five, and started to school. He and his older brothers and sister walked to the nearby Pleasant Grove School. Malcolm also started going with his father to U.N.I.A. meetings. His proudest memory of his father was hearing him speak at these meetings, which always ended with him saying, "Up, you mighty race, you can accomplish what you will."

Earl Little was still harrassed by white townspeople. This and other problems caused friction between Malcolm's parents. After an argument one day, Earl Little angrily stormed out of the house. The next thing the family heard was that he had been run over by a streetcar. People in the black community blamed white racists. The life insurance company refused to pay death benefits, saying that Earl Little had caused his own death.

Malcolm was six when his father died. His mother tried to care for her large family, but with so many mouths to feed, sometimes the children were so hungry they got dizzy. Malcolm got into the habit of visiting family friends at dinner time, hoping they would invite him to eat. By the time he was nine, he started stealing apples and other food from stores.

When he got caught, the state welfare workers wanted to put him in a foster home, but he was sent to live in the home of one of the families he had visited at dinner time, then to a detention home after being expelled from school.

Malcolm was taken to the detention home by a social worker who encouraged him to turn his life around. Malcolm took this advice seriously. He did well while at the detention home. He attended Mason Junior High School. He was a member of the debating society, and on the basketball team. His grades were among the highest in school, and he was elected seventh-grade class president.

A turning point came one afternoon when a teacher asked Malcolm what kind of career he would like. Malcolm hadn't really thought much about his future, but replied that he would like to become a lawyer. The teacher said that was an unrealistic goal for a black person, and suggested that Malcolm become a carpenter.

Malcolm's hopes were shattered. In his *Autobiography*, he noted, "It was then that I began to change—inside." He began to draw away from white people and he lost interest in school. He went to live with a half sister, Ella, in Boston. She was one of the children from his father's first marriage, and Malcolm had been impressed with Ella when he first met her. "She was

Malcolm X

the first really proud black woman I had ever seen in my life."

Life in Boston was totally different from anything Malcolm had known before. Up to this point he had never smoked, gambled, or had a sip of liquor. Before long he tried all of those things. He got a job at a pool hall and met a fellow nicknamed "Shorty," who was also from Lansing, Michigan. With Shorty's help, he got a job as shoeshine boy at the Roseland State Ballroom where the big bands played. He developed a love of music, and enjoyed meeting Duke Ellington, Count Basie, and other big band leaders. But he started staying out all night with Shorty and his friends and was soon caught up in a life he would later regret.

Shorty's crowd called him "Red" because of the reddish color of his hair, which he had had "conked" or straightened. He bought a zoot suit with a long coat and a gold chain. He frequented black bars and pool halls, was outstanding on the dance floor, and soon found that he could make extra money by dealing in drugs. He did things he later was ashamed of, especially his disrespect for women.

His sister Ella suggested that he get a job on the railroad. She thought this would get him away from his Boston lifestyle. Malcolm got a job on a train that ran between Boston and New York City—and discovered Harlem. "This world was where I belonged."

He had heard that Harlem was the most exciting black community imaginable, and he found it fascinating. He got so caught up in the excitement that he hardly took time to sleep. Back at his job on the train, he was rude to customers and ended up getting fired, but he got hired at Small's Paradise, a restaurant and nightclub which was one of the most popular gathering places in Harlem.

It was while working at Small's that Malcolm got a new name. To distinguish himself from other red-headed young men in Harlem, he called himself "Detroit Red" because he was from Michigan. He liked his job and was a good waiter. He earned large tips, but gambled away his money as fast as he earned it and ended up getting fired. Some of his customers were gamblers and gangsters, and he had learned the tricks of their trade. He was into drugs in a big way, and selling them was so dangerous he started carrying a gun. After a while, the police watched him so closely he could hardly make any sales. He got deeper and deeper into criminal life, going from one illegal hustle or money-making scheme to another. He and another fellow began robbing houses.

Shorty took him back to Boston, and there Malcolm organized a burglary ring, was quickly caught, and sent to Charlestown State Prison. He was only twenty years old.

In prison he got a new nickname—Satan—because he was considered mean and evil. Then he met a prisoner who was an avid reader and could command respect of both prisoners and guards by his skillful use of words. Malcolm was encouraged to make use of the prison library and he took some correpondence courses, even one in Latin. As he said in his *Autobiography* ". . . the streets had erased everything I'd learned in school." Now, the more he learned, the more he wanted to learn.

His brothers and sisters had kept in touch, and after being

transferred to Concord Prison, Malcolm got a letter from his brother Reginald, who told Malcolm that if he stopped eating pork and smoking cigarettes, he could get him out of prison. Malcolm couldn't imagine what that had to do with it, but he was eager to find out. Reginald came to visit him, but instead of telling Malcolm more about getting out of prison, he told him about Elijah Muhammad, leader of the Nation of Islam, whose followers were called Muslims. Reginald urged Malcolm to join, as he and other brothers and sisters had done.

Malcolm pondered on what he was told. One of Elijah Muhammad's teachings was that any of the problems black people had resulted from laws passed or actions taken by white people. Another was that followers should not smoke or eat pork. In some ways, the Nation of Islam's message was similar to the words he had heard from his father at U.N.I.A. meetings years before.

He could be accepted in the Nation of Islam, even with his criminal past. He felt guilty about many of the things he had done and welcomed this chance to have a new start in life. He wrote to his brothers and sisters, to Elijah Muhammad, and others. This was the first time he tried to write anything since school days, and he realized he needed to improve his reading and writing skills. He figured out a way to do both. "I saw that the best thing I could do was get hold of a dictionary—to study, to learn some words."

He patiently copied everything printed on every page of the dictionary, using a pencil and a lined writing tablet. He memorized the meanings of words that were new to him. He learned about people and places and events in history. He began reading on every possible subject. In his cell at night, he read by the light that came in underneath the door.

Malcolm realized that history books he had in school did not include much about Africa or African-American history. He felt that every student should know about the national and international contributions of Africans and of blacks in America. His broad interests prepared him to take part in the prison's debating program and he became an excellent debater. He also became a student of the teachings of Elijah Muhammad. He used his skills to convert many of his fellow prisoners to the Nation of Islam.

Upon his release from prison, Malcolm went to Michigan to live with his brother Wilbert, whose family belonged to the Nation of Islam in Detroit. The more he learned about the Nation of Islam, the more impressed he became. He especially admired its teachings of self-esteem, discipline, and respect for women.

Malcom was overjoyed when he had the opportunity to meet Elijah Muhammad. He offered to recruit new members after work at a job at the furniture store where his brother worked. He was formally accepted into the Nation of Islam and he, like other members of the group, used "X" as a last name to replace slave names. Sometimes he addressed the meetings at the Nation of Islam temple.

Elijah Muhammad recognized Malcolm's potential. He proved to be such an effective recruiter and speaker that he soon was made assistant minister at the temple. Then Elijah chose him to be the national spokesman and chief minister. The

Nation of Islam grew rapidly, largely due to the efforts of Malcolm X. Audiences were sometimes 10,000 people. Schools were established and a newspaper, *Muhammad Speaks*, was started. Members were taught "to do for self" and not to depend on others. White Americans had created many of the problems black people encountered, but starting with African civilizations, black people had demonstrated their ability to be self-sufficient.

Malcolm X established temples in Boston, Philadelphia, and New York. He was a popular speaker wherever he went. He was known for his keen knowledge of many subjects, quick wit, and anger about the suffering of his parents and other African Americans. He spoke on college campuses, and was often interviewed by magazines, television, and newspaper reporters. His future wife, Betty, attended his lectures and was attracted by his clean-cut appearance and his no-nonsense manner. Although Malcolm had mistreated women when he was younger, he would take marriage and, later, fatherhood, very seriously.

Civil rights marches and sit-ins were being held in the South at this time. Dr. Martin Luther King, Jr., was conducting non-violent demonstrations so that black people could vote and use public accommodations. Civil rights workers were sometimes injured by white people who wished to deny them those rights. It was not the policy of the Nation of Islam to be involved with the marches and sit-ins. However, Malcolm X thought that if the security units of the Nation of Islam could go into the South, it would discourage violence to civil rights workers. He and Dr. King were both dedicated to improving the lives of

African Americans, though they differed on how to reach that goal.

At this time, Elijah Muhammad was having health problems. Influenced by some ministers who resented Malcolm's power and position, his attitude toward him changed. Elijah Muhammad became convinced that Malcolm X was trying to take over the organization. The strained relationship between the two was intensified when Elijah objected to public comments Malcolm X made about the assassination of President John F. Kennedy. The result was that Elijah Muhammad forbid Malcolm X to speak in public for three months.

Even after the silencing, Malcolm X was still dedicated to the Nation of Islam. He and his family visited Florida where he helped a young prizefighter named Cassius Clay mentally prepare for the World Heavyweight Championship fight. Cassius Clay won the fight, then announced that he had become a Muslim and was changing his name to Muhammad Ali. When Malcolm returned to New York, he found himself cut off from the Nation of Islam.

He considered his next move. In his *Autobiography,* he wrote that "My life was inseparably committed to the American black man's struggle . . . Now, I had to honestly ask myself what I could offer." He decided to organize the Muslim Mosque, Inc. in New York City. This organization would welcome black men and women from all faiths and all walks of life.

Malcolm X had one thing to do before he could devote all his time to his new Mosque. For many years he had known that the teachings of Elijah Muhammad were different from the religion of Islam as practiced elsewhere. He would make

Dr. Martin Luther King, Jr. (left) and Malcolm X

his *hajj* or pilgrimage to Mecca, the holy city in Saudi Arabia, and learn more about the Islamic religion. Following this, Malcolm's name became El-Hajj Malik El Shabazz, which denoted that he had made his *hajj*.

He met pilgrims from all over the world and discovered that differences of skin color and language were not barriers. For the first time, he lived without racial prejudice. He began to rethink his views on race, knowing that this would surprise everyone who knew him. He began to feel hopeful that someday blacks and whites could live peacefully together.

He believed it was important to establish a link between Africans and African Americans. He considered getting black people to think on a global scale to be one of his major accomplishments. He traveled to a number of African countries, and often he was asked about race relations in the United States. Some people he met had read newspaper reports of lynchings and beatings of civil rights workers. He became convinced that human rights violations of black Americans should be brought before the United Nations.

Back in the United States, Malcolm X formed the Organization of Afro-American Unity to help Afro-Americans in attaining human rights. He felt there had to be black solidarity before there could be black and white unity. He felt an urgency about his work. He had received death threats, and wanted to accomplish as much as he could.

Malcolm X was in Africa when the racial disturbances of the summer of 1964 reached their peak. Upon his return to New York, many well-wishers greeted him at the airport. New death threats also awaited him. So did a court order of eviction from the home he and his wife believed to be a gift from Elijah Muhammad.

Attempting to continue his work, he traveled to several cities in the United States. Following a brief trip to Europe, he returned to New York on Saturday, February 13. Early the next morning he and his family were awakened by an explosion and fire in their home. It reminded Malcolm of the terrifying experience he had had as a child. As he told Alex Haley, to whom he dictated his life story, "I don't expect to live long enough to see my book published."

On Sunday, February 21, 1965, Malcolm X went to the Audubon Ballroom to speak to a meeting of his Organization of Afro-American Unity. As he greeted his listeners, he was shot and killed by gunmen in the audience. His wife, Betty Shabazz, and their four daughters looked on in horror.

Newspapers in every major capital in the world carried accounts of the assassination of Malcolm X. Radio and television stations interrupted their programs to announce his death. At the funeral, actor Ossie Davis delivered the eulogy: ". . . Malcolm was our manhood . . . in honoring him, we honor the best in ourselves . . ."

As the procession of funeral cars drove the eighteen miles from Faith Temple in New York City to Ferncliff Cemetery in Westchester County, black people all along the route paid their final respects by placing their hands or hats over their hearts. Twenty years earlier, Malcolm would not have received any such tribute. In the intervening years he had grown and changed so markedly that he will long be remembered.

Where There's a Will, There's a Way

CAST

Mrs. Walton	Al
Brenda	Maria
Louis	Kareem
Rhonda	Narrator

Needed items: Dictionaries in the students' desks. Chalk and chalkboard or marker and large sheet of paper.

NARRATOR: We join Mrs. Walton's class in the midst of a discussion.

MRS. WALTON (*to class*): You have just read the life story of Malcolm X, and you know that when Malcolm was in prison he found a unique way to improve his reading and writing skills. What type of book did he use to accomplish this?

LOUIS: A dictionary.

MRS. WALTON: That's right. As you know, that proved to be the ideal tool. Why?

BRENDA: A dictionary is full of words.

RHONDA: So are other books.

BRENDA: What I mean is that dictionaries list words and then explain the meaning of each word. When Malcolm got through reading and copying down that whole book, he must have known a little bit about everything.

LOUIS: He sure did! He was a debater and he gave great speeches. Nobody could have done all the things he did without knowing lots of words.

MRS. WALTON: What are some of the subjects Malcolm X could have learned about from the dictionary?

BRENDA: All of them.

MRS. WALTON: Malcom X often debated about politics, religion, and law. Do you think he learned anything about those subjects from the dictionary?

AL: Yes, he could learn some things about them by finding out what those words mean.

MARIA: All those subjects use a lot of big words. The dictionary told what those big words meant.

KAREEM: That's what he needed to know first if he wanted to study those subjects.

MRS. WALTON: What other kinds of information could he have gotten by reading the dictionary?

NARRATOR: One by one, the students take out their dictionaries and page through them as the discussion continues. Mrs. Walton picks up a piece of chalk and writes her students' answers on the board.

BRENDA: He could have learned about all kinds of things—like plants and animals.

RHONDA: He could have learned the names of different countries and where they are. If his dictionary had a map he could have found where each country is.

LOUIS: Malcolm X could have learned about math. You can find the words "add" and "subtract" and "multiply."

KAREEM: He could have learned about the planets, the stars, and the moon.

MARIA: . . . and about man-made things that fly in the air, like rockets, airplanes, balloons . . .

AL: Don't forget sports. He could have read about baseball, basketball, football, soccer. And games like checkers and dominoes.

BRENDA: Music is another thing he could have read about. There are pictures of musical instruments in the dictionary.

RHONDA: I never stopped to think much about what is in a dictionary before. One thing nobody else mentioned is that a dictionary shows you how to pronounce and spell words. Of course, you have to have some idea of how the word is spelled in order to look it up.

AL: That's true, but speaking of ideas, the dictionary explains the ideas behind different inventions. Malcolm must have read about them, too.

MRS. WALTON: Of course, he read many other books after he read the dictionary, but the dictionary got him off to a good start.

LOUIS: Malcolm X was one smart man!

KAREEM: He sure was.

Author's Note

I had at least one unique experience connected in some way with every person featured in *Follow in Their Footsteps*. Some were the result of my research, others were wonderful unforeseeable surprises.

During the writing of the Carter G. Woodson chapter, I met and interviewed Dr. Woodson's niece, Mrs. Marion Pryde, and Miss Lena Miles, who knew and worked with him. While attending the 75th anniversary convention of the Association for the Study of Afro-American Life and History in Chicago, I met Sister Scally, who wrote the book about Dr. Woodson. In a presentation where I introduced the skit which accompanies the Woodson biography, I randomly selected people in the audience to play various roles. To my amazement, one of the people who in the skit pretends to be a child that walked to the Phillis Wheatley YWCA with Dr. Woodson actually had been one of those children.

When Dorothy Height was in Chicago for the first Black Family Reunion to be held there, she agreed to meet with me. Although I had read everything I could find about her, she filled in details and told me things that were not included in the materials. In talking with her, I learned how she got her middle name, how she chanced to learn of the scholarhip that allowed her to develop her potential, and how hard she had to work to get it.

There were family-related Baltimore connections when I wrote about Thurgood Marshall. My father, whose name was John L. Tilley, Sr., had conducted a highly successful voter registration campaign in Thurgood Marshall's hometown. He knew Thurgood Marshall and what it meant for him to win the Brown vs. Board of Education case. Mrs. Thelma Rice, a college friend of my mother, knew Mrs. Ivora Gibson, a childhood classmate of Thurgood Marshall. It was she who remembered how their teacher used to let him conduct mock trials in their classroom.

Knowing that Bessie Coleman's international pilot's license was in the DuSable Museum in Chicago, I went to see it. There I talked with Miss Theresa Christopher and she suggested that I contact Bessie Coleman's niece, Ms. Marion Coleman. It was a thrill to hear Ms. Coleman tell about her family memories. She enlisted my help in trying to get a U.S. postage stamp issued in honor of Bessie Coleman, and she and I were both in attendance at the dedication ceremonies for the Bessie Coleman Public Library in Chicago and for the U.S. postage stamp.

I was fortunate to be able to consult with Rufus A. Hunt, a pilot and an expert on African Americans in aviation. He led the flyover honoring Bessie Coleman and was very gracious and patient in explaining pertinent details and technicalities. I subsequently wrote the Bessie Coleman entry in the *Chicago Women's Encyclopedia*.

Through a series of coincidences I got to meet and talk with Alex Haley. While doing research on Frederick Douglass at the Maryland Hall of Records for *Take a Walk in Their Shoes,* I had met Mrs. Phebe Jacobsen, the person who helped Alex Haley find information about the ship Kunta Kinte arrived on. Later, while working on the Haley material, I knew that his last book, *A Different Kind of Christmas,* was about the Underground Railroad. Since I had done extensive research on the Underground Railroad in Illinois, Pat Scheffler, host of a local cable television program, invited me to appear on a program with Alex Haley. He had agreed to let me interview him next time he was in town, but said that he would be arriving just before giving a lecture and leaving soon afterwards. If he had a few minutes, he would talk with me.

He had to leave as soon as the lecture was over, but I caught up with him as he went to catch the limousine that was to take him back to the airport. When I expressed my disappointment that we hadn't had a chance to talk, he said, "Come ride out to the airport with me. We can talk on the way." So Alex, the limousine driver, and I set out, and I got my interview.

The day after Alex Haley died I bought copies of all the newspapers, so I could read their accounts of his life. I went to a restaurant to read them over a cup of coffee and ran into Ernie and Caroline Gibson, friends whom I had known for years. They asked me to join them, and I learned that they had known Alex Haley's father but the topic had just never come up in any of our previous conversations.

My friends, the Gibsons, were also connected with another person featured in this book, A. G. Gaston. They had been the managers of the Gaston Motel and Restaurant at the height of the Civil Rights Movement. When Dr. Martin Luther King, Jr., went to Birmingham during that period, Mrs. Gibson was the one who met him at the airport.

Charlemae Rollins was a member of the Children's Reading Roundtable of Chicago when I joined back in the early 1970s. She was well loved and respected by many other librarians like Zena Sutherland, Annie Lee Carroll, Dorothy Evans, and Doris Saunders, who shared their personal memories of Charlemae with me. The professional staff of the ALSC division of ALA was wonderful about supplying information from their resources.

In writing Charlemae's biography, I had the full cooperation of her son, Joe Rollins. He sometimes telephoned me from his home in the Bahamas, and when he attended the Charlemae Rollins Colloquium in Durham, North Carolina, he brought me photographs of his mother, knowing I would also be there. And a high point for me was the day that the Charlemae Hill Rollins Children's Room was dedicated at the Hall Branch Library. I was on a panel with Augusta Baker, Janet Del Negro, Annie Lee Carroll, and Ginny Moore Kruse. The audience consisted of all the children's librarians in Chicago.

I knew that some of Edmonia Lewis' sculptures were at the National Gallery of Art in Washington, D.C. I was in Washington to attend a conference, but the sessions were scheduled so close together that I didn't have a chance to get to the Gallery. When the conference ended, I was to visit a cousin, Elsie Wallace. Without knowing about my wish to go to the National Gallery of Art, she suggested that we go there. I not only got to see the Edmonia Lewis sculptures but learned about the techniques used by sculptors. Esme Bahn, Dorothy Porter, and Marilyn Richardson were all extraordinarily helpful in unlocking the mysteries of Edmonia Lewis's life.

Some years ago, Jean Meehan, a neighbor who knew of my long-standing interest in the Underground Railroad suggested that I visit the Raleigh Township Museum in North Buxton, Ontario, Canada. Arlie Robbins was the curator there and had grown up with a deep interest in the history of the area. She had gathered information about the Shadd family and other black families that settled there and took great pride in showing me Mary Ann Shadd Cary's printing press. Prior to that visit, I had not realized how significant a historical figure Mary Ann Shadd had been. I was delighted to include her biography in *Follow in Their Footsteps*.

I met three people who knew Malcolm X very well, and who had different perspectives on his life and work. First of all, I heard Betty Shabazz speak about her husband and met her afterwards. Although I did not get to interview her personally, I read articles in which she was interviewed. I met and talked with Alex Haley, who had interviewed Malcolm X extensively for his autobiography. The third person was Dr. John Henrik Clarke, who did historical research for Malcolm X when he was preparing for radio and television interviews.

These are some of the memorable things that happened to me during the writing of the biographies and skits in this book. Each helped me gain new insights about the people who are featured and enriched my life in other ways.

—GLENNETTE TILLEY TURNER

Index

Page references in italics indicate illustrations